Lacan
A Beginner's Guide

ONEWORLD BEGINNER'S GUIDES combine an original, inventive, and engaging approach with expert analysis on subjects ranging from art and history to religion and politics, and everything in-between. Innovative and affordable, books in the series are perfect for anyone curious about the way the world works and the big ideas of our time.

aesthetics	engineering	NATO
africa	the english civil wars	the new testament
american politics	the enlightenment	nietzsche
anarchism	epistemology	nineteenth-century art
ancient philosophy	ethics	the northern ireland conflict
animal behaviour	the european union	nutrition
anthropology	evolution	oil
anti-capitalism	evolutionary psychology	opera
aquinas	existentialism	the palestine–israeli conflict
archaeology	fair trade	parapsychology
art	feminism	particle physics
artificial intelligence	forensic science	paul
the baha'i faith	french literature	philosophy
the beat generation	the french revolution	philosophy of mind
the bible	genetics	philosophy of religion
biodiversity	global terrorism	philosophy of science
bioterror & biowarfare	hinduism	planet earth
the brain	history	postmodernism
british politics	the history of medicine	psychology
the Buddha	history of science	quantum physics
cancer	homer	the qur'an
censorship	humanism	racism
christianity	huxley	rawls
civil liberties	international relations	reductionism
classical music	iran	religion
climate change	islamic philosophy	renaissance art
cloning	the islamic veil	the roman empire
the cold war	journalism	the russian revolution
conservation	judaism	shakespeare
crimes against humanity	justice	shi'i islam
criminal psychology	lacan	the small arms trade
critical thinking	life in the universe	stalin
the crusades	literary theory	sufism
daoism	machiavelli	the torah
democracy	mafia & organized crime	the united nations
descartes	magic	the victorians
dewey	marx	volcanoes
dyslexia	medieval philosophy	the world trade organization
economics	the middle east	war
energy	modern slavery	world war II

Beginners
GUIDES

Lacan
A Beginner's Guide

Lionel Bailly

ONEWORLD

A Oneworld Paperback Original

Published by Oneworld Publications 2009

Reprinted 2013, 2017, 2018, 2020

Copyright © Lionel Bailly 2009

The right of Lionel Bailly to be identified as the Author of this
work has been asserted by him in accordance with the
Copyright, Designs and Patents Act 1988

ISBN 978–1–85168–637–7
eISBN 978–1–78074–162–8

Typeset by Jayvee, Trivandrum, India
Cover design by www.fatfacedesign.com
Printed and bound in Great Britain by Clays Ltd, Elcograf S.p.A.

Oneworld Publications
10 Bloomsbury Street
London WC1B 3SR
England
www.oneworld-publications.com

Stay up to date with the latest books,
special offers, and exclusive content from
Oneworld with our newsletter

Sign up on our website
www.oneworld-publications.com

MIX
Paper from
responsible sources
FSC® C018072

Contents

Illustrations

Acknowledgment

When I asked Sham Ambiavagar to edit this book, it was still in the form of an early draft and much of what I had intended for it was drawn from my years of lecturing on the subject, from my own analysis, and from my clinical practice. Sham's questions highlighted occasional weaknesses in the Lacanian edifice or in my understanding of it; however, as a non-clinician, her research was book-based and her understandings derived by a mixture of insight and logic, rather than clinical experience. Her argumentative approach forced me to account for what my years of Lacanian practice revealed of the theory – and it seems to me that many of Lacan's greatest insights were intuitive and clinically derived, and not logical philosophical constructs. Sham's insistence upon *attempting* a unified theory, whether or not one may indeed be arrived at, has also contributed to the readability of the final product, although I would not wish to pretend that there are no holes in it, which hopefully will continue to attract constructive contributions. In addition, my mother tongue is French and I speak English, while hers is English and she can speak French. We had to negotiate over the meaning of words and the impossibility or unhelpfulness of direct translation. This led us sometimes to unusual ways of translating concepts or fragments of texts, which I think are useful as they preserve the French meaning better than exact translations, which do not work in the spirit of English. Overall, the process of working with Sham was unexpectedly rich and complex and without it this book would not exist.

Introduction

Jacques Lacan was first of all a psychiatrist, and as a clinician, he was more concerned with what he did not know or understand than what he did. His inability to 'make do' with a poor explanation led him to consider and explore all models available to psychiatrists in the first part of the twentieth century. After having worked with some of the most brilliant proponents of organic psychiatry, he found in psychoanalysis the most helpful theoretical model to understand and treat the complex patients he was dealing with. However, Lacan was to become more than just a disciple of Freud: he believed that Freudian theory was not a perfect edifice but a work in progress, and wanted to contribute towards what he saw as a developing model. His attitude towards the development of theory was modern in that he was willing to examine any body of science that could clarify or shed new light on the phenomena he was trying to explain, and consequently, he drew inspiration from biological psychiatry, genetic psychology, and philosophy; later, structural linguistics, anthropology, and even mathematics joined the range of theoretical models he used.

The result was extraordinary, and its richness has attracted students in fields far from psychoanalysis or psychiatry; indeed, although Lacan's model is not a philosophical one, it has become most fashionable among students of philosophy: one could go so far as to say that in the English-speaking world, it is largely philosophers and academics in English and Critical Studies departments who have kept Lacanian thought alive. Certainly, in the field from which Lacan himself came – that of psychiatry – his work is mostly ignored. This may be because philosophers and academics in the humanities are, in one respect, better equipped to deal with his writings than students of psychiatry or psychology: they are better prepared to try to understand a thinker whose productions are sometimes irritatingly obscure. There are three reasons behind the obscurity, which arise mostly from the manner in which Lacanian theory was formulated.

Most Lacanian theory has been gathered from Lacan's spoken teachings; his technique was that of the philosophers of the classical world, who expounded and developed their ideas in a discourse with their pupils; he wrote very little for publication. In even the most lucid speaker, transcriptions from speech are often problematic; the speech of a man who engaged his audience by many means other than pure logical exposition becomes quite obscure when written down. In order to make his points, Lacan often relied on dramatic devices (the well-timed pause, the leaving of a half-finished thought hanging in the air …), the impact of his own personality, and perhaps most of all, on the ability of his audience to arrive *of their own accord* at the desired conclusion (by making the final mental connections themselves, as one should in analysis) – and this mode of expression makes frustrating reading. The only writings Lacan can be held responsible for are his *Ecrits*, which were, it seems, rather painfully extracted from him by a publisher in 1966;[1] in these, he maintains his abstruse, suggestive style – leading the reader towards an idea, but never becoming absolutely explicit, unless by means of a 'matheme' (see below). I would also suggest that Lacan's impenetrable style was due, surprisingly, to a kind of intellectual caution, which made him wary of making sloppy and indefensible pronouncements, and that his fear of being misconstrued, coupled with a natural ineptness in communication, led to him literally tying his meanings up in verbal knots, hedging about every half-statement with half a dozen qualifying sub-clauses, and obsessively weighing each and every word.

Secondly, the controversy that surrounded his working life and the strong passions he engendered in his followers and detractors have made it quite difficult to discover what he actually said: Lacan became mythologised, even when he was alive. His seminars – the main arena in which he expounded his ideas – were inherited by Jacques-Alain Miller, his son-in-law and disciple, who has kept tight control over their release. Some of his most important ideas have never been published, but are only referred to in other works. Also, he thought on his feet – the ideas expounded in his seminars were never intended to be cast in stone – and there are contradictions and discrepancies in his recorded utterances – recorded, it must be noted, by faithful followers subject to their own preconceptions and interpretations.

Thirdly, Lacan was an inventor of concepts and freely ascribes to common words new meanings within his theoretical model – just as would a philosopher, or, for that matter, any inventor. Accordingly, in order to understand his theory, readers must learn to accept new definitions for words, and drop the assumptions they may already have; acquiring the Lacanian vocabulary is a prerequisite for being able to understand his theoretical models, particularly as they became more and more complex, building upon concepts he invented and named. This is an intellectual approach that students of philosophy are perhaps more used to than medical students, and which may explain why Lacanian ideas are more often discussed in humanities departments of universities than in a clinical context.

This is a pity, because Lacan's work, like Freud's, is *not* philosophy, but a meta-psychology – a theoretical framework within which to understand the individual. It is best understood in the context of a therapeutic relationship between an analysand and an analyst: in other words, a patient and a therapist. This is why students of pure philosophy may have problems with central Lacanian concepts – *they have not witnessed in a patient what he is talking about*; it is also why clinical practitioners may be able to grasp and apply his concepts intuitively, while being quite unable to explain them in logical terms. Lacan, despite the fuzziness of his communication style, strove desperately hard for intellectual rigour; it was perhaps this that made his relationship with words so fraught, and it was certainly this that drove him increasingly towards mathematical formulae to express without ambiguity what he meant; but at the end of the day, it is not pure logic but clinical relevance that validates Lacan's model, and this book attempts to bridge the gap between the two.

Author's note

As this book is intended for readers without a background in psychoanalysis or psychology, I have introduced concepts early on by way of some deliberate over-simplifications, and then built upon the understandings so conveyed with the addition of layers of complexity; I hope that at the end, what is gained by the reader will be a relatively faithful understanding of his ideas. For the sake of clarity, I have capitalised certain words, which Lacan never did – Real, Imaginary, Symbolic, Subject, Phallus; this is to avoid any even fleeting ambiguity, as these words also have other commonplace meanings that may intrude as a distraction. By capitalising these words, I wish to designate these particular, Lacanian meanings, so that I may use the words with their other meanings, uncapitalised, without risk of confusion.

1

Lacan in his historical context

If the 1890s saw the birth of psychoanalysis, then the 1920s saw it reach a kind of adolescence, where across Europe, it was breaking free of its parental boundaries and seeking its place in the wider intellectual world. As an attractive and intriguing newcomer, it was courted by many different, older disciplines – medicine, art, literature – whose practitioners took it up with enthusiasm, used and abused it, gossiped about, and fought over it. Equally, it worried others in those and other fields, who felt it to be an upstart threat. Psychoanalysis itself, with the promiscuous spirit of exploration and creativity of youth, absorbed far-reaching and sometimes unexpected influences: from the surrealists, from linguists, from poets. In Paris, the 1920s also saw the intellectual blossoming of a generation of young psychiatrists whose relationship with the new science (to use the word in its broad sense) was to lay the foundations of French psychoanalysis as it is today.

Psychoanalysis in France had different roots from its Viennese parent: Viennese psychoanalysis grew up with middle-class neurotics on the couch; French psychoanalysis grew up with psychotic patients in the bleak wards of mental asylums. It was also something of a late developer, with the medical establishment there not really taking the new ideas into their bosom until the 1920s. Then, at St. Anne's Hospital in Paris – the French capital's main mental hospital – two departmental heads, Gaëtan de Clérambault (at the l'Infirmerie Psychiatrique de la Préfecture de Police) and Henri Claude, began to have a far-reaching impact on the development of psychoanalysis in their country. The contribution of the former was accidental – Clérambault himself never 'took' to the new idea – but Henri Claude was enthusiastic about it, and in his unit at St. Anne Hospital, an analysand of Freud's, Eugénie Sokolnicka, was allowed to analyse the younger psychiatrists. With Claude's encouragement, many of these people – or their own analysands – were to become the founder members of the French psychoanalytic movement, René Laforgue, Edouard Pichon, René Allendy, and Sophie Morgenstern among them. In 1926, under the firmly steering hand of Princess Marie Bonaparte, they founded the Société Psychanalytique de Paris (SPP), which became the most important psychoanalytical organisation in France, and remains one of the two French groups officially affiliated to the International Psychoanalytic Association (IPA).

Clérambault was a controversial figure because of his eccentric and difficult personality, and had no time for psychoanalysis, but he was an extraordinary clinician whose detailed descriptions of psychotic symptoms still form a benchmark of clinical excellence. In his first psychiatric work, *L'Automatisme mental*, written in 1909, Clérambault suggested that the mechanism of 'mental automatism' – when the mind appears to work independently of conscious control – might be responsible for 'experiences of hallucination'. He divided mental automatism into three types: associative, sensory, and motor. Associative automatism includes disturbances in the form of thought (such as hallucinatory thoughts that occur as if you have no control over them); sensory automatism manifests itself as unpleasant feelings in internal organs thought to be caused by somebody else; and motor automatism involves the delusional belief that somebody else performs one's movement and actions.

Clérambault also left his name to a form of paranoid disorder – the delusion of being loved-now known among English speakers as Clérambault's syndrome, 'Erotomanic Delusion' or 'Erotomania'. He described this condition in 1927 as *psychose passionelle*, a sort of passionate psychosis, which takes the form of a paranoid delusion with an amorous quality. He noted that the patient was usually a woman who had developed a delusional belief that a man, with whom she may have had little or virtually no contact, was in love with her. The person selected was usually of a much higher social status and thus was likely to be unattainable as a love object.

The brilliance of Clérambault's clinical work left a deep impression on the mind of a young trainee in his unit: Jacques Lacan, who was to adapt his style of meticulous clinical observation to psychoanalysis.

The formative years

At the outset, Lacan's intellectual journey was that of many of the founder members of the French psychoanalytic movement: he began his studies at the faculty of medicine in Paris and completed his psychiatric training (between 1927 and 1931) at St. Anne's, under Clérambault and Claude, with whom he had good relationships. But he was a few years younger than these founding members – twenty-five when the SPP was founded – and he had to wait several years before he could attain membership of the group; his place in this inner circle of the SPP elite was, from the start, semi-detached.

French psychoanalysis was closely linked with medical psychiatry, and its proponents were dealing with extreme cases: the people treated by Clérambault, Claude, and by Lacan and his contemporaries would have been suffering from acute and chronic psychosis and manic depression. In addition, in 1930, Lacan spent two months at the Burghölzli – a mental asylum in Zurich which had been established in the 1860s as a model of the new, 'humane' way of treating severe mental cases. Here, he worked under Hans Wolfgang Maier, successor to its most illustrious director, Eugen Bleuler.

Bleuler (whose assistant was Carl Jung) belonged to the generation that presided over the birth of psychoanalysis; he took Freud's ideas from the domain of neurosis into psychosis, challenging the prevailing belief that psychosis was the result of organic brain damage, insisting that it could have psychological causes, and trying to use the mechanisms described by Freud to understand it. In 1911, he wrote in *Dementia praecox oder Gruppen der Schizophrenien* (Dementia Praecox or the Group of Schizophrenia): 'I call dementia praecox "schizophrenia" because (as I hope to demonstrate) the "splitting" of the different psychic functions is one of its most important characteristics. For the sake of convenience, I use the word in the singular although it is apparent that the group includes several diseases.' Bleuler believed that delusion could be meaningful, even in psychosis: for example, an auditory delusion – the hearing of voices – could be seen as an internal discourse which has a relation to the subject. This view, novel then, has become widely accepted; it was also to remain lodged as the germ of an idea in the mind of Jacques Lacan. Bleuler also coined the term 'Autism' by the contraction of **Aut**o-Erot**ism**.

Upon his return to Paris, Lacan completed his medical thesis – a work which bears deeply the marks of the men who trained him. *De la psychose paranoiaque dans ses rapports avec la personnalité* (Of Paranoid Psychosis and its Relationship with the Personality), presented in 1932, contains a case study of a woman suffering from Clérambault's 'passionate psychosis' of erotomania, and incorporates Bleuler's ideas of the meaningfulness of delusion. However, '*Le Cas Aimée*' (The Case of Aimée), as it is commonly referred to, does more than merely reproduce the ideas of his teachers: one can see in it already that Lacan was drawing inspiration from unusual sources (see below – *Surrealism*).

Shortly after presenting this thesis, Lacan began his own analysis with Rudolph Loewenstein, a Polish-born analyst who was one of the founding members of the SPP; Loewenstein's analyst was Hans Sachs, an important Viennese member of the IPA, and one of Freud's disciples. Loewenstein was a very 'orthodox' analyst and the relationship between Loewenstein and Lacan was somewhat conflictual: it seems that, privately, Loewenstein questioned Lacan's analysability and Lacan, Loewenstein's talent. Lacan had, perhaps, already too many ideas of his own.

In 1934, Lacan applied for membership of the SPP and was given 'candidate member' status; he was granted full membership four years later. In 1936, at the International Psychoanalytical Association meeting at Marienbad, Lacan presented his first paper, 'The Mirror Stage'.[1] Here, the tension between Lacan and the psychoanalytic establishment was apparent: he resented being stopped by Ernest Jones because the ten minutes given to his presentation were up. There was probably fault on both sides: in the establishment, for not recognising the importance of Lacan's presentation sufficiently to grant him some leeway, and in Lacan for 'not playing the game' when he was such a newcomer. But the incident, and Lacan's huffy reaction to it, shows his self-belief, which some call arrogance: he had a great idea of himself, and could not bear being treated like a minor player. However, hindsight also shows that he was *right* to believe in the extraordinary nature of his work, for out of everything presented at that conference, 'The Mirror Stage' remains the most important work.

From the 1920s onwards, Lacan moved in avant-garde intellectual circles, befriending the writers André Breton and Georges Bataille. André Breton was one of the leaders of French surrealism, having written the Surrealist Manifesto in 1924, while Georges Bataille's writings were more abstractly philosophical: he developed the concept of base materialism, which had an influence on the deconstructivist thinking of Jacques Derrida. Lacan also associated with Salvador Dali and Pablo Picasso, whom he greatly admired, and several of his articles were published in the surrealist magazine, *Minotaure*.

In 1938 Lacan received his full membership of the SPP; this was also a year in which the shadow of war was heavy over Europe. Freud and others of the Viennese circle were helped to safety in England, and stopped on their way in Paris. Much is made by historians of the fact that Lacan was absent from the evening organised by Marie Bonaparte to receive the Viennese – and of Lacan's later claim that he had decided not to go to it because he did not want 'to please Marie Bonaparte'. In reality, it is far more likely that the young psychiatrist and new SPP member was simply not invited, and his glossing over of this is an indication that Lacan was vulnerable to narcissistic hurt.

One major impact of the war on the evolution of psycho-analysis was the transfer from Europe to the English-speaking world of the majority of its leading lights. Even before the war, there had been tension between the American Psychoanalytical Association (APA) and the IPA, with the Americans wanting to accredit only analysts with a medical training, and the Europeans wishing to keep the new discipline quite separate from medicine. The dominant psychological model of the United States was at the time (and is still today) the Behaviourism of Edward Lee Thorndike, John B. Watson, and B.F. Skinner; the APA, with their insistence upon a medical degree, clearly thought it necessary to present psychoanalysis with the same trappings of science – or at least as something that could be assessed and regulated in the same way as a science.

When the Nazis dissolved the Viennese Association, there was a general exodus of intellectuals from Europe to Britain and the United States. Sigmund Freud died in London in 1939; his daughter Anna and disciple Melanie Klein remained working there for the rest of their lives. Even more significantly, Heinz

Hartmann, Ernst Kris, and Rudolph Loewenstein (who had tried to analyse Lacan) fled to the States, where they were to become the founders of Ego Psychology – a branch of psycho-analysis that drifted rapidly towards the functionalist thinking of much modern psychology. European psychologists without a psychoanalytical background also fled to America; they included Wolfgang Köhler and Max Wertheimer, who joined their colleague Koffka to become the founders of Gestalt Psychology, which gave rise to Cognitive Psychology.

While psychoanalysis lay dormant in Europe under Nazi rule, east coast America and London became the centres of its development. London played host to most of the Viennese 'old guard'; it also may have had some of the most gifted theoreti-cians, but the United States had more wealth and therefore, more power. In London, Ernest Jones tried to hold out against the American drive for control of the IPA, but it was a losing battle; in a meeting just after the war, he had to agree to a 'power-sharing' arrangement in which the presidency of the IPA would alternate between Europe and the States. This arrange-ment was reached between seven Americans and six members of the British Society: no other European organisation was party to it; the Americans had, in fact, achieved a 'coup' in the absence of all other European representation. From this point onwards, the issue of the regulation and accreditation (and therefore train-ing) of psychoanalysts was to dominate the further development of the discipline in the manner of a straitjacket.

How did the war affect Lacan? For him, the war years were a silent period: he published nothing in this time, and remained working as a psychiatrist at the military hospital of Val de Grace in Paris. What he did in the immediate aftermath suggests that silence for Lacan did not mean intellectual dormancy; the prolif-eration and maturity of his immediate post-war presentations suggest that the war years had been a time of intense reflection. But what he was able to observe of the evolution of the rest of the psychoanalytic community during this period may have been less than congenial to him.

One does not know how much information he received from the United Kingdom and America during the war, but in its aftermath, Lacan would have seen that the psychoanalytical writings emanating from the other side of the Atlantic were developing into Ego Psychology and Gestalt Psychology, which were irrelevant to his thinking. Immediately after the end of the war (autumn 1945), he spent five months in England, ostensibly studying the English practice of psychiatry in war-time; but one wonders how much this visit was motivated by a curiosity about developments in psychoanalysis in the city in which Sigmund Freud had died, and which was now home to his most direct heirs.

The very next year, Lacan began again to present psychoanalytical papers: that he had continued to think, and perhaps to write in private, during the occupation, is evidenced by his presentation of six papers in the space of a year. Lacan's production continued to be prodigious in the coming years – mostly in the form of presentations. The return to France of Claude Lévi-Strauss in 1948, after years in the Americas, provided a fresh stimulus to his thinking: Lévi-Strauss's development of structural anthropology led Lacan to use Saussurian linguistics in the same way.

Lacan was now attracting a following: the younger analysts in particular were excited by his new ideas, which were developing in counter-current to developments in the English-speaking world. Some of Lacan's more provocative formulations can be best understood in the context of a challenge to the increasing tendency to treat psychoanalysis – and psychology – as subject to simple scientific proofs. France was not immune to the formalising tendency – in order to be accepted by the IPA, the SPP had to produce a system of accreditation, and a training programme to go with it. By 1949, Jacques Lacan had a central role in the formulation of this programme – but as always, his relationship with other leading SPP figures was uneasy.

Institutional battles

The Lacanian innovation that caused the greatest problem for the SPP was his use of sessions of variable duration, which have come to be known as 'short sessions'. In classical psychoanalysis, clinical sessions between the patient and analyst last just under an hour, and this was a duration fixed upon by the IPA in their phase of rule-making. Lacan's sessions lasted, according to Elizabeth Roudinesco, between ten and forty minutes, with an average of twenty minutes. The short sessions were seen as problematic by the analytical establishment for more than one reason. Firstly, the sessions represented a transgression of the IPA rule; secondly, the IPA were afraid that this practice would put the analyst in an omnipotent position; thirdly, and maybe most importantly, it allowed Lacan to accept many more trainees than the other training analysts. The risk was that after a few years of this regime, Lacan would command the loyalty of a majority of the newly trained psychoanalysts. Lacan's adherence to this technique was to cause him problems with the entire psychoanalytical establishment for the rest of his life, but in the early 1950s, the causes of tension between him and the other leading SPP members were more general and political.

The wider context in which the SPP power-struggles of the day must be seen was created by the seizure of power by the American movement at the end of the war, and their insistence upon regulating training and accreditation. The IPA now insisted upon a formalised system of accreditation, and the SPP, if it wished to retain IPA recognition, had to produce a set of rules in line with IPA thinking. In the early 1950s, two currents started to emerge within the SPP: on one side, the 'conservatives', who favoured the medical model and were keen to create an institute of psychoanalysis in order to implement IPA standards of training; and on the other, the 'liberals', who preferred a more psychological model and opposed the rigidity of the planned institute. Despite being a doctor himself, Lacan sided with the 'liberals', and ironically, it was almost immediately after he had become president of the SPP that he resigned from it.

In June 1953, a small group of 'liberals', led by Daniel Lagache, walked out of the SPP to set up an alternative society, the Société Française de Psychanalyse (SFP); Lacan quickly joined them. The new SFP now had to negotiate its recognition from the IPA, and in doing so, fell into the same trap its members had experienced while still in the SPP: the need to demonstrate to the IPA that its standards of training followed IPA rules. Predictably, it was Lacan's use of 'short sessions' that provoked the crisis. At its annual meeting in London in 1953, the IPA refused the affiliation of the SFP and asked a committee to examine their application. This fact-finding commission was directed by Winnicott and its members were the American psychoanalyst, Phyllis Greenacre, a friend of Anna Freud's, Willi Hoffer, and Jeanne Lampl De Groot, a Dutch analyst trained by Freud.

None of this appeared to dampen Lacan's morale; if anything, during the period in which the SFP was under the surveillance of the IPA committee, the energy with which he continued to develop and disseminate his theories increased. Immediately after the schism with the SPP, he presented his paper 'The Symbolic, the Imaginary and the Real' at St. Anne Hospital; two months later, in Rome, he delivered 'The Function and Field of Speech and Language in Psychoanalysis'. In November, he gave a public seminar – the first of a series that was to continue for twenty-seven years.

For the duration of this first IPA investigation, the problem of the variable duration sessions just would not go away: Lacan would not renounce them, and the IPA would never accept them. He continued to practise in this way while publicly denying it: he told representatives of the IPA that he was following their rules, but regulatory bodies hate transgressors, and hate transgressors who show contempt even more. What happened next was quite shocking to the French psychoanalytical movement – particularly to members who had grown up with the easy freedom of the developing discipline in its formative years.

The committee's views on Lacan were negative in many more ways than expected: not only did they find him to be using 'short sessions', they also felt that he was very 'seductive' towards his pupils: he had an influence on trainees that was judged to be too great and probably unhealthy. The committee also criticised the child psychoanalyst, Françoise Dolto – not as an analyst, but as a training analyst. They felt that she lacked method and that she was often the object of a 'wild transference' by her pupils; the committee was afraid that she would 'influence the young generation'. The findings of this committee, therefore, meant that two of France's most respected and influential psychoanalysts would not have professional recognition as training analysts.

The discrepancy between the hostility Lacan attracted from critics and the status he held in the eyes of his admirers posed a great problem for the international regulators. The negotiation between the SFP and the IPA went on, and in July 1959, the executive committee of the IPA decided to create a new committee to re-examine the application of the French association. In May 1961, Pierre Turquet, Paula Heimann, Ilse Hellman, and Pieter Jan van der Leeuw arrived in Paris to interrogate members of the SFP, whom they divided into a senior and a junior group. The negotiation took place between May 1961 and December 1963. But already, at the start of the process, following the commission's first series of interviews in May–June 1961, the IPA executive committee had recommended that Lacan should not be allowed to take on any new training cases.

None of this made any difference to Lacan, to his developing ideas, or to his students, who continued to flock to his seminars. These were the arena in which he expounded his theories, and became the basis of the Lacanian canon. It is essential to bear in mind that much of the apparent obscurity of Lacanian theory, as well as much of the provocative quality of his statements, comes from the simple fact that his theory was not recorded in the cool consideration of the act of writing, but from the interactive and audience-dependent form of oral teachings. This gives the learning of Lacanian theory its special flavour – his ideas were developed in the ancient discursive style, by speaking out loud to an audience, and receiving their reactions – the modus operandi of the ancient Greek and Roman philosophers, or of scholars at the medieval universities. Lacan's theory has been transcribed from seminars in which his articulations push the audience towards the understanding of a concept, towards a moment where there is something of a feeling of epiphany, in which the listener comes to a realisation, and this in turn has earned him the negative epithet of 'guru'. 'Guru-ism' is intellectually suspect because it suggests that the 'disciples' have been duped or seduced into an irrational belief; however, all theoreticians are as guilty of such seduction – and it is even more often carried out by apparently rationalist and speciously scientific means.

Lacan's mode of communication was effective for his audience because it employed the device of 'realisation': just as in analysis, an individual has to arrive at a realisation by him/herself, and that realisation has a force far greater than if it was received as 'information' from another party. Lacan led his audience, sometimes by provocation, sometimes by fuzziness, to think along a certain path until they reached of their own accord the conclusion he wished to bring them to. It is not surprising, therefore, that those who understood/understand him did/do so with such belief and conviction – they have experienced inwardly the truth of what he said: it carries the 'force of realisation'. However, while this style of communication worked well in his seminars, when transcribed onto the page, it has led to misunderstandings, irritation, or disgust – very often because few people bother to read the thing in its entirety, or they are presented with the few provocative statements he came out with, quite out of context.

Lacan's academic career appeared to progress undisturbed by the lack of formal recognition: in 1964, he was appointed part-time lecturer at the Ecole des Hautes Etudes, and editor of the Champ Freudien series. But the very same year, the IPA commission concluded their report, and in August told Lacan that he would be struck off the IPA's list of training analysts that October. Lacan promptly resigned from both the IPA and the SFP.

There had been dissent within the SFP over Lacan's intransi-gence for some time: some members wanted international recog-nition more badly than others and felt that Lacan should make some concessions – in particular drop his use of short sessions – in order to remain within the fold of the IPA. When the SFP was dissolved, those members created the Association Psychanalytique de France (APF), while those 'loyal' to Lacan joined him in setting up the Ecole Freudienne de Paris (EFP), on 21 June 1964. This was soon to devise its own training programme.

The inquiry and 'trial' of Jacques Lacan split the French psychoanalytical world. Lacan's attitude and behaviour towards the IPA was arrogant and childish: he called the Turquet Commission the 'turkey commission'; he lied to them about his use of short sessions, as if it really did not matter. But the commission's manner was perhaps equally childish: the grounds upon which they recommended his expulsion were all to do with their judgements upon his personality. At no point was there ever any discussion or debate around the theoretical basis of his ideas, his teaching, or his use of short sessions; indeed, given that it was as a training analyst that Lacan was expelled, it is startling how little theory was ever mentioned. Even more remarkable is the fact that, after Lacan's expulsion, the leading lights of French psychoanalysis, to a man accepted by the IPA – Jean Laplanche, Jean-Bertrand Pontalis, Didier Anzieu, and Daniel Widlöcher – were all trained by Lacan; Daniel Widlöcher even became its president. The IPA did not seem to see the irony of expelling someone as a bad trainer and then appointing one of his trainees as their president.

Lacan's oppositional attitude towards the IPA was perhaps more than merely childish: he did really seem to believe that the kind of regulation they sought to impose was fundamentally wrong: that psychoanalysis, still a young and evolving field of work, should not be bound by the strictures imposed by any group of people. Freud, he liked to point out, was never dogmatic: his theory *and his practice* continued to change and develop until the end of his life. This, according to Lacan, was how psychoanalysis had to be. One can look at the history of almost any science or humanity or art, and see how fixed and accepted views that were paradigmatic for a generation, or even a millennium, have bitten the dust; and yet, just decades after the birth of psychoanalysis, a group of disciples of Freud had gone down the road of dogma, in a manner whose closest parallel can only be found in religion.

With the expulsion of Lacan from any internationally recognised body, the schism in French psychoanalysis seemed set in stone, with its two alternative institutions as irreconcilable as the Catholic and Protestant churches. But Lacan, the 'antipope', seemed only to be gaining in strength; paradoxically, he was even becoming popular in intellectual circles in the United States, where the interest showed in him by students of literature and philosophy almost matched the disdain shown by their colleagues in psychology.

In 1966, he addressed a colloquium at Johns Hopkins University. In 1968, a group of Lacanian-trained analysts set up a Department of Psychoanalysis at the University of Vincennes

(Paris VIII); Lacan became its scientific director in 1974. The following year, he was invited to lecture at Yale and MIT. In 1980, the year before his death, Lacan dissolved the EFP and set up in its place the Ecole de la Cause Freudienne. He died at the age of eighty, having lived to see that his work would survive him for a very long time, and still without 'accreditation' from the IPA: perhaps he wanted to prove his own dictum true – that 'the psychoanalyst derives his authorisation only from himself'.

Lacan's intellectual journey

Creative thinking draws from many different sources, in what has become commonly known as lateral thinking, which simply means being open to ideas from varied sources and having the intellectual capacity to see the relevance of one in another. The practitioners of a new science or art form are especially free to draw together ideas from different disciplines in the development of their own; some cross-fertilisations are less successful than others. One of the founder members of the SPP, René Allendy, was an adherent of homeopathy, numerology, and esotericism; Carl Jung turned to alchemy and folklore for inspiration. Time is the best test of the worth of ideas, and now, Jacques Lacan's nose for the intellectual *Zeitgeist* appears unerring: he chose fields of study that remain within the mainstream of intellectual activity, and focused on innovations within those fields that are still respected today.

Surrealism

Lacan's medical thesis, in which he presents at length the case of a deluded woman who attempted to stab a famous actress, drew on the work of the surrealists. In particular, he was struck by an article written by Salvador Dali in which the artist described how some of his images were obtained by 'un processus nettement paranoïaque' – 'a clearly paranoid process' – in other words, Dali's images are created by the same mental process by which paranoid delusions are produced. An example of this is the transformation of a verbal metaphor into a concrete object: the idea of someone 'bending over backwards' to do something may conjure an image of someone literally doubled over backwards, as if their spine was articulated the wrong way – the kind of image that could appear in a dream, a surrealist painting, or a paranoid delusion. Lacan married the Bleulerian notion that delusions have the meaning of an 'internal discourse' with their subject with Dali's observations on his creative process and reflected upon the process by which the delusion/dream image is produced through an interpretation of reality by means of language.

Philosophy

From an early age, Lacan had taken an interest in philosophy; the staunch Catholicism inculcated in him by his mother (he went to a Jesuit school) was eroded by his love of Spinoza; it is perhaps the influence of Spinoza's monism (the belief that there is no duality between mind and matter, that there is a single driving principle behind phenomena, and that everything is reducible to mathematical formulae) that gave him his lifelong conviction of the inseparability of affect and intelligence, or the wrongness of compartmentalisation as a means of understanding. In his love of philosophy, Lacan was drawn naturally towards a systematisation of thinking and the construction of paradigms; he also fell into the philosopher's habit of procuring common words and affixing to them meanings relevant to a new paradigm – a habit that makes Lacan easily misunderstandable by readers who have not made the same intellectual journey.

To Lacan, mastery of the philosophical method was so essential that after finishing his medical studies, in the period in which his theoretical innovations were coming to a boil, he took on a private tutor to give him a crash course in philosophy, and attended the seminars of Alexandre Koyré and Alexandre Kojéve, who introduced him to the philosophy of Hegel, Heidegger, and Husserl. The work of Husserl in particular led Lacan to an intense reflection about the concept of ego, alter ego (the other), consciousness, etc., and led directly to his formulations of the Subject, the Other (*le grand autre*), and later to the 'Name-of-the-Father'. Likewise, his interest in Platonic forms led to his formulation of the Real and the Imaginary.

Psychology

Henri Wallon (1879–1962) was a psychologist who also based much of his thinking on philosophical models, and in particular Marxist and Hegelian dialecticism. Not only did Wallon share Lacan's love of philosophy, but he was also one of the very few authors of that time who tried to cross-fertilise psychology and psychoanalysis.

Wallon used this methodology in his conceptualisation of childhood development as a dialectical relationship between affectivity and intelligence, which underpin the development of the child. This means that at any one time, both affectivity and intelligence are at play, but with one predominating over the other. This model allows for the possibility of regression, and differs greatly from that of the other great founder of developmental psychology, Jean Piaget, who compartmentalised development into cognitive, social, and emotional spheres, and whose views of development are more linear. Wallon found this kind of compartmentalisation unhelpful, and insisted instead upon a kind of horizontal linkage between different areas of development within a developmental stage. He believed also in a discontinuity between stages, and that these discontinuities were triggered by crises. Wallon put a strong emphasis on the role of language and the social milieu in understanding the development of the child. He also defined five principal stages in the child's development, in each of which affectivity and intelligence play greater or lesser roles: the *impulsive and emotional stages* (0 to 3 months), the *sensorimotor and projective stage* (1 to 3 years), the *personalism stage* (3 to 6 years), the *categorial stage* (6 to 11 years) and the *adolescence stage* which begins after 11 years.

Lacan met Wallon socially in 1930, and Wallonian thinking played an early role in the development of Lacan's theory. Wallon wrote about 'the symbol' and 'the image' in connection with the development of the child's psyche; Lacan was to build upon that to arrive at his conception of 'the Symbolic, the Imaginary and the Real'. In addition, Wallon's *Les Origines du caractère chez l'enfant*, published in 1934, developed themes such as the prematurity of the human baby, transitivism, and the other, and also contained twenty pages devoted to the baby and the image in the mirror – all ideas that became central to Lacanian thinking.

Lacan was asked by Wallon to write a chapter in the *Encyclopédie française*, and his article, 'Les Complexes familiaux', published in 1938, is clearly influenced by Wallon's thinking. Among the Wallonian ideas he uses are those of functional anticipation, the role of proprioception (the perception of the position and movements of the body) in the construction of body image, and that the recognition of oneself in the mirror comes at the start of the process whereby the child develops from merely perceiving images to affixing labels and meanings to them – the 'passage from image to symbol'. More famously, Lacan's founding work, 'The Mirror Stage' (1936), borrowed and modified the Wallonian concept of the mirror test where a child between six and eight months old manages to recognise itself in the mirror.

Linguistics and structuralism

Linguistics was another fast-developing field from which Lacan borrowed ideas, and his 'borrowings' here were inspired by the work of social anthropologists, who had done it first. Early in the twentieth century, the Swiss linguist Ferdinand de Saussure's innovative course at Geneva overturned the orthodox views of German philology (the study of the historical development and morphology of languages) and laid the basis for a new approach, not just to linguistics, but to anthropology and sociology as well. Saussure had been a part of the movement that launched the investigation of the Asiatic origins of European languages.

Saussure rejected the positivist conception of language as one of simple correspondence to the physical world. The relationship *between words* is of greater importance than the relationship between words and objects. It is the relation of the Sign (the word) to the code of signification (the language) that accords it meaning, rather than a simple correspondence with an external object. Saussure showed, through looking at linguistic variation and innovation, that distinctions within the language had a knock-on effect upon other terms, tenses, prefixes, etc., which meant that any singular innovation necessarily impacted upon the whole code of language or its structure (hence his linguistics being called 'structural'). For Saussure, language was studied not as a tool or medium, but an object of study in its own right. One of Saussure's innovations in linguistics that was to become central to Lacanian conception and practice was his analysis of the relationship between signifiers (words) and the signified (meaning).

Claude Lévi-Strauss saw parallels between Saussure's findings in linguistics and recent developments in anthropology –

another new and labile 'science', which was still in the process of separating fully from its parent disciplines of sociology and ethnology. At the time, anthropology was drawing heavily on the 'functionalist' sociology of Emile Durkheim, and using it to look at the rituals, taboos, and mores of primitive societies from the standpoint of their functionality to those societies. This approach to anthropology was pioneered by Durkheim's nephew, Marcel Mauss, who employed it in his study of the nature and function of sacrifice, and in his famous essay on the role of symbolic gifts amongst Native Americans (*Essai sur le don*, 1924).

Lévi-Strauss was not satisfied with the functionalist approach in anthropology, which involved isolating particular institutions and trying to find parallels between those and modern institutions (for example, Azande witchcraft is 'their version' of medicine), as it implied looking at other cultures simply as versions of our own. Lévi-Strauss realised that Saussure's approach allowed him to go further than Durkheim's functionalism, and to look at culture in itself as a code of meaning. Just as Saussure came to his linguistic codes by studying the relationship between the elements of language, Lévi-Strauss tried to find the code that underlies and links the elements within a culture – for instance, the way that a culture's mores and taboos interact and support each other.

The literary critic Roland Barthes extended the analysis of codes of signification developed by Levi-Strauss and Saussure to analyse popular culture. In his hands, Saussure and Lévi-Strauss's structuralism became a full-blown 'science of signs' or semiology. Barthes reversed the commonsense view that authors wrote texts, to argue – cryptically – that texts 'wrote' authors. The slogan of semiotics became 'The death of the author'.

By the mid 1940s, Lacan had already discovered the relevance of Saussurian linguistics in the formulations of his theories of psychoanalytical practice – one of his first presentations after the war showed that he had been reflecting upon how meaning is encoded in the speech of the analysand in a way that escapes the consciousness of the speaker. In the 1950s and 1960s, Lacan took up Lévi-Strauss's method, 'structuralism', and used it to examine how not just language and culture but individuals themselves could be seen as a code of meaning in Saussure's sense; and as Barthes argued that texts 'wrote' authors, Lacan argued that 'discourse writes the Subject'.

Also drawing on Saussure, Lacan proposed that in the Subject's unconscious, the relationship of words one to another is of greater importance than the relationship of a word to an object. Another of his theories was that 'the unconscious is structured like a language' – which has sometimes been misunderstood as the unconscious being structured *by* language. Lacan's insight here is that of an experienced clinician: he saw that the encoding of meanings in dream images followed the same rules as the encoding of meaning in language. This allowed him to 'read' dreams by their Subjects' discourse about them.

Mathematics

Lacan always had a rather difficult relationship with language, in the sense that he could not express himself clearly; when asked as a young doctor to write an encyclopaedic article, 'Les Complexes familiaux', his original text was sent back many times for correction, because it was so unclear. When reading his works, one gets a sense of how very cautious he always was in his choice of words – too cautious: every statement is hedged around by half a dozen qualifying sub-clauses, which in turn allow for multiple digressions, and make following the main point of a sentence difficult. But the impression one receives is that this obscurity is, strangely, the product of a fear of saying something wrong; it is perhaps this worry that led him to immerse himself in mathematical formulae, in which he hoped to find clearer expression.

Lacan was fascinated by the eighteenth-century mathematician, Desargues, and also Leibniz, who developed topological models. Lacan always seemed to find such figures easy ways of envisaging a problem, and towards the end of his career, his use of topology became more and more complex, so that by his last seminars, they had become his main mode of expression of his ideas.

Topology is the branch of mathematics that studies the properties of a space that are preserved under continuous deformations; because it involves finding properties that remain constant no matter how much the *appearance* of the space changes, it is an attractive model for a psychoanalyst looking for consistency of factors in the bewildering complexity of the human psyche and its interactions. Lacan felt that by expressing psychological patterns in mathematical figures, he could make the relationships between different elements easier to envisage. We all do this to some degree – an everyday example is when we use the term 'a triangular relationship' to describe one in which the dynamic of emotion depends upon three parties.

Lacan's topological models were more complex, and towards the end, highly complex. One of his best known and most useful is that of the moebius strip, which he used to describe the relationship between the conscious and unconscious in the construction of the Subject. The moebius strip is a continuous loop with only one surface, but which nonetheless presents a back and a front (a visible and an invisible) aspect, showing the singularity of the Subject in an apparently dualistic system.

Lacan also used the theory of knots to express the relationship between the Imaginary, the Symbolic and the Real. He also used algebraic notation to construct 'mathemes' – formulae for expressing psychoanalytical concepts. The first and most famous of these was when he overturned the Saussurian algorithm by writing:

$\underline{S}$ (signifier)
$\overline{s}$ (signified)

to express the relationship between the signifier and the signified in the functioning of the psyche.

While Lacan's mathematical elaborations are difficult to follow to the point of impracticality, they were paradoxically born of a desire for clarity: they were aimed at reducing the dependency of psychoanalysis upon intuition, by the production of models that could work quite independently of the talents and personality of the analyst. They also had a didactic purpose: Lacan wanted his theories to be transmitted accurately and independently of the variations and nuances that may be created by the imaginations of teacher and pupil.

His mathemes and topological models were perhaps Lacan's philosopher's stone: the point in his quest at which his ambition surpassed good sense; or perhaps he simply did not live long enough to refine his method to a point at which these things become useful, because they remain mainly of rather esoteric academic interest.

2
Through the looking glass
The Mirror Stage

Unable as yet to walk or to stand up, and held tightly as he is by some support, human or artificial, he nevertheless overcomes, in a flutter of jubilant activity, the obstructions of his support, and fixing his attitude in a slightly leaning forward position ... brings back an instantaneous aspect of the image.

('The Mirror Stage', own translation)

One of Jacques Lacan's key preoccupations was the development of the individual human psyche as a whole entity comprising inseparable conscious and unconscious elements; in Lacanian terms, the 'birth of the Subject'. The Lacanian concept of 'Subject', in striking evolutionary similarity with any real human subject, remained to the end elusive, but became over the decades more and more layered, subtle, and complex. It is a lodestone within his work, much of which is directed at trying to define it.

The English word 'identity' is defined by the *Oxford English Dictionary* as 'the sameness of a person or thing at all times or in all circumstances; the condition or fact that a person or thing is itself and not something else; the condition or fact of remaining the same person throughout the various phases of existence; continuity of the personality'. While this may be the closest commonplace equivalent of Lacan's Subject, the latter depends on the user accepting that there are elements of one's identity of which one is unconscious; anyone who thinks that one's identity is only what one wishes to say about oneself ('*I am Irish, I am an independent career woman*', etc.) is talking about what Lacan would have called the ego. Lacan's Subject is composed of and revealed by signifiers, which it utters without knowing what they mean.

His further elaborations of the Subject will be seen in later chapters of this book, but the keynote and most accessible work remains his first original contribution to psychoanalysis, 'The Mirror Stage' (1936). The Mirror Stage has to do with the first time the child thinks of itself as 'I' in relationship with an image that it starts to understand as representing itself.

As developmental psychologist Henri Wallon pointed out, the human baby is very premature at birth compared with other animals, including the higher primates. From birth up until maybe eighteen or more months, the infant is unable to stand up, walk, or handle objects with dexterity, and the sense of 'self' and 'wholeness' that is allowed by mature proprioception (perception of the whole body within its environment) is absent. However, this human baby – immature, helpless, perceiving itself only in a fragmented way – is, at some point between the ages of six and eighteen months, going to see an image in the mirror, and realise that it is itself. This will be the first time the baby discovers itself as a unitary being, and this discovery is the source of an intense feeling of joy and excitement, which is usually shared with the adult present; the infant, having made this discovery, turns back to look at its mother, for example, and shares with her its pride and surprise. This founding act, leading to the formation of the ego and the perception of the Subject, is attended by powerful emotion.

Lacan said: 'we have to understand the mirror stage as an identification ... the transformation that takes place in the subject when he assumes an image'. The baby's discovery of self is an intellectual act: it involves the translation of an image into an idea – the idea of 'me' or 'self'; hence, human identity is based on a primary act of intellect. But this is not a restatement of Descartes's *cogito ergo sum*: I think, therefore I am. Indeed, Lacan was completely opposed to 'any philosophy issuing directly from the cogito':[1] for him, the opposite was true – *I think, therefore I am not*, or *I am fully a subject only when I am not thinking* – the very act of thinking about oneself nullifies the Subject. This is something that will be explained later.

While identifying itself in the mirror, the child also identifies with something from which it is separated: it is as an 'other' that the Subject identifies and experiences itself first. The founding act of identity is therefore not just emotional and intellectual, it is also schismatic, separating the Subject from itself into an object. For Lacan, the Mirror Stage is 'the symbolic matrix in which the I is precipitated in a primordial form, prior to it being objectified in the dialectic of identification[2] with the other, and before language restores to it, in the universal, its function as subject'.[3] At the Mirror Stage, the intellectual perception of oneself is an alienating experience and the beginning of a series of untruths; but it is a necessary alienation that allows the Subject access to the symbolic realm.

The specular or mirror image is a lure: an unreal character that is also symmetrically opposed to reality (right becomes left and vice versa). Before the Mirror Stage, the child was already able to recognise other people in the mirror – its mother, its brother, another child ... it could recognise the image of another fellow human before recognising its own: this means that it arrives at the Mirror Stage with prior knowledge of the false nature of the image. When it finally recognises itself in the mirror, the child *already knows* that this image is not 'the real person'; unlike a monkey, who may try to attack the image as a rival, the baby understands almost immediately its unreality, while experiencing powerfully *through* this unreality the whole-ness of itself for the first time – '*this is not me, and yet this is me*'.

From the beginning, the child's identity (or Subject) is both '*what I am*' and '*what others and I see of me*' – the image *is* oneself and simultaneously *not* oneself, and no sooner has there been this splitting, than there is a merging and confusion of subject and object – an 'adoption' by the Subject of its objectified image. For the infant, the image of itself is fascinating – the starting point of a life-long reflection upon itself. This implies that the foundation stone of the human Subject or identity is an intellectual, schismatic act of narcissism.

'Narcissism' is a term that in common parlance has the negative connotation of vanity; however, its meaning in psychoanalysis is closer to 'a beloved view of oneself' – the foundation stone essential to the development of identity/Subject. This view is necessarily beloved, not because it is always a very positive view, but because without it, identity crumbles: an attack on one's narcissism is usually very powerfully experienced and may threaten the whole edifice of Subject. This is perhaps why it is observable that infants and small children have such a strong response to those who look most like themselves, and that response has to be 'mastered' as love or be recognised as hate. It seems to be, among very young children, that it is the small differences that exist between oneself and someone very similar that are least tolerated, perhaps because they raise the question of 'which is the authentic version?' which seems to attack the whole artifice of ego. The Mirror Stage points up the fundamental place of narcissism in the creation of identity/Subject – the seeing oneself *as* an image, and the love of the image that *is* oneself.

The value of this understanding in psychoanalytical practice is manifold; Lacan's emphasis upon the formation of this notion of 'I' – the Subject – underpins the whole of his conception of psychoanalytical process. 'The function of the Mirror Stage ... is to establish a relation between the organism and its reality'[4]; this intellectual relationship of the Subject's internal world and the external world is the beginning of consciousness of self as an object, and because of the mental process of translating the image into a concept of 'self', it is also the beginning of the submission of the subjective self to processes of symbolisation.

Lacan first introduced 'The Mirror Stage' at the International Congress of Psychoanalysis at Marienbad in 1936 and then developed it further to underpin his concepts of Subject and Other, which form the basis of Lacanian psychoanalytical practice. He expounded these further developments at the sixteenth International Congress of Psychoanalysis in Zurich in 1949, where he explained that 'it [the Mirror Stage] sheds light on the formation of the *I* as we experience it in psychoanalysis'.

Lacan said of the idea of whole self precipitated by the baby's encounter with its mirror image:

> This form would have to be called the Ideal-I ... it will also be the root stock of secondary identifications ... this form situates the agency known as the ego prior to its social determination in a fictional direction that will forever remain irreducible for any single individual, or rather, that will only asymptotically approach the subject's becoming, no matter how successful the dialectical synthesis by which he must resolve, as I, his discordance with his own reality.[5]

In defining the Lacanian Subject, one has to look first at what was unsatisfactory to Lacan in the formulations of ego and id; in order to do this, one must go back to the development of those terms. Lacan did not seek to contradict Freud: he always said he wanted to restore him. It must be remembered that Freud never coined the terms 'ego', 'superego', and 'id'. He always wrote '*das Ich*', '*uber-ich*', and '*das Es*', which would translate simply and straightforwardly as 'the I', 'super-I' or 'over-I', and 'the It'; in France, this was translated as '*le moi*', '*le sur-moi*', and '*le ça*'. Freud was very anxious about translations of his works, and his fears were well-founded. The first of his books to be translated into English, *The Interpretation of Dreams*, contained his first formulations of '*das Ich*'. Abraham Brill, the translator, was a Galician-born doctor who had a personal connection with Freud and attended his lectures, and who had emigrated to the United States, but whose native language was not English. Freud thought that he would be a 'safer bet' as a translator, nonethe-less, because he knew him.

However, Brill's substitution of the Latin 'ego' for '*das Ich*' immediately deprived it of the emotional and completely personal force of a simple 'I'; Brill and subsequent translators did not see that the subjectivity inherent in '*Ich*' was important, or that its everyday plainness was a defence against the facile affix-ing to it of corrupting meanings. Commonplace and emotion-ally loaded words such as 'I' cannot be redefined or given new meanings; one can only seek to describe and explain them better, with all the caution and intense reflection that this requires. The choice of 'ego' – void of commonplace meaning – meant that it could be quickly filled with new meanings that innovators in the English-speaking psychoanalytical world might wish to affix to it; moreover, the little meaning it *did* have (for those with schoolboy Latin) was the derisory one of self-centredness and being puffed up. This was a bad beginning for the nascent concept; 'ego' was simply too weak to defend itself against appropriation. This danger was recognised even at the time: when James and Alix Strachey came to write their standard translation of *Das Ich und das Es*, their publisher, Leonard Woolf, voiced his preference for a more straightforward 'The I and the It'; he was over-ruled – not by the Stracheys, who had reserva-tions themselves about these words, but by those who wanted 'technical terms' for the new 'science'. The outcome was that, within thirty years of coming into existence, *ego* had broken far away from *das Ich*, and Ego Psychology had affixed definitions and qualities to the 'technical term' drawn heavily from

Behaviourism, which would probably have dismayed Freud, and distanced it from the simple fact of a person upon a couch saying 'I'.

Lacan, while aware of the developments in psychoanalysis taking place in the English-speaking world, would have been less affected by the evolution of *ego*; however, in French too, '*le moi*', while being closer to the original, has the problem of being the *objective* case of the first person pronoun: it has lost the subjectivity of '*je*'. From Lacan's point of view, '*le moi*' falls into precisely the trap set for the Subject at the point of its first apprehension of itself in the mirror: it sees itself as an 'other', and it seeks to describe and define itself as it does others, with a tool (language) that is quite beyond its control, creating, as it does so, a smokescreen of lies. As Joël Dor points out: 'The subject's imaginary objectivation of himself is called the ego (le moi)'; and 'the ego (le moi) takes itself for the I'.[6] Lacan sought to restore the subjectivity of '*das Ich*', or '*je*' as opposed to '*moi*' – the subjectivity of the person whose discourse he hears.

The making of '*le moi*'

After the primary act of self-recognition, in which the baby has identified itself as an Ideal-I in the mirror, the elaboration of the ego comes with the gradual acquisition of language. The baby sees in the mirror the object that is itself, and hears its mother name it: *Tom, Ellie*, etc. It has heard its name before, of course, but now, it affixes it to the image in the mirror, and can first begin to formulate: that's Tom/Ellie, that's *me*. 'Me' is the objective case of the personal pronoun and very shortly after it has seen itself as an object, the child begins to attribute traits and characteristics to this 'me'; through identification with the image, the individual speaks as an actor would. Sometimes, the child, when it begins to speak, refers to itself in the objective

case, 'me' before it learns to use the subjective 'I': *me hungry* ...
or sometimes even more objectively in the third person: *Ellie
want telly, Tom's ball!* When not using 'me' or its given name,
the child will get around the mystery of 'I' by avoiding pronouns
altogether: *not tired*, etc. comes before *I'm not tired.* The infant's
habit of referring to itself in the third person or by the objective
pronoun suggests the *méconnaissance* of, or obliviousness to, the
Subject, which in that initial act of self-recognition, has been
overlaid by the object-image: it is only through the object-
image that the child can speak of itself; and yet simultaneously,
it is that unrecognised Subject who is speaking.

Méconnaissance is a French word encompassing non-recogni-
tion of and obliviousness to something; it is sometimes translated
as 'misrecognition' – a translation I find goes wide of the mark.
'Misrecognition' suggests that something has been recognised,
only wrongly. In my preferred translation of *obliviousness* or *non-
recognition*, the subject is completely blind to the object. One of
Lacan's most important maxims is that human beings are very
largely oblivious of their own Subject; the ego is what a person
says of him/herself; the Subject is the unrecognised self that is
speaking. Psychoanalysis is about accompanying the patient
towards his/her subjective truth, or towards the point where the
objective 'me' and the subjective 'I' can be united.

Lacan insists upon the fictional nature of the ego – fictional
in both the original sense of 'that which is fashioned/framed'
and its common sense of 'an imaginary narrative': the Mirror
Stage situates the ego 'before its social determination in a
fictional direction ... he [the baby] must resolve as *I* his discor-
dance with his own reality'. He held that the ego was not based
on a 'perception-consciousness system or organised by the
reality principle', but existed instead by 'the function of *méconnaissance*'. As the child's language develops, it begins to attach
ideas to the objectified self, which is to become the ego or
'*le moi*': the ideas it attaches are often produced by a denial of

reality, denegation, or wishful-thinking. The three year old who cries, '*Race you, Daddy! I'm winning!*' is showing his/her desire to win, in the face of an easily observed reality – that Daddy's legs are four times longer and much faster. The father is likely, for his part, to let the child win – precisely because he wishes to help the development of the *child's image of itself* as a winner; he is, in fact, aiding and abetting the fiction of his child's ego (in this case a necessary defence against the anxiety of being so small and helpless). And this fiction is maintained and nurtured throughout one's life; denegation too helps: '*I've got no problem with so-and-so*' is almost always a contradiction of the truth; but it helps the speaker maintain his/her fiction that she/he is easygoing/unaffected by the so-and-so in question.

The factitious, 'created' nature of the ego is behind Lacan's opposition to 'any philosophy directly issuing from the Cogito': the *cogito* of Cartesian thinking relies mostly on the status of consciousness – the status in which the ego believes itself most to be in control. But for Lacan, the real 'I' is the Subject – *I* in 'I am' – and this is necessarily hidden by conscious thought about itself. At the Mirror Stage, one may think of the Subject as the part that 'invents' the stories about its image-self or ego, affixing to it signifiers as it acquires language: *girl, blonde, pretty, likes chocolate, hates pink, good at drawing*, etc.; but it also represses as many signifiers as it selects, and in doing so, tries to hide something of itself. Indeed, the Subject can only come into being when it is not thinking, because the very act of any thinking that involves its ego creates a smokescreen behind which it disappears.

Other mirrors

During the baby's first recognition of itself in the mirror, and because of its helplessness at this stage, it is usually not alone. In his description of the Mirror Stage, Lacan has the infant

supported by an adult (the mother) who has probably introduced it to the mirror; she anticipates the importance for the
baby of solving this puzzling situation, and is rarely silent. She
talks to the child, often guiding it: '*Look, who is that in the mirror?*'
In this emotion-laden exchange, the child is overwhelmed with
the excitement of suddenly realising who the image represents,
and turns back to look at its mother: its victory is dedicated to
her, it wants to share the triumph with her. Often, the mother
confirms the baby's discovery in a form that uses its name:
'*That's John in the mirror!*' – a formulation that suggests the image
in the mirror is a double, another baby, and reinforces the baby's
own perception of itself as an object.

The involvement of the mother in the child's conquest of
identity is not surprising. Indeed, since the child's birth, the
mirror phase has been anticipated within the relationship
between the baby and its mother: the gaze of the mother is the
first mirror in which the child is faced with the issue of its image
– that is, what the mother sees. Before the Mirror Stage, the
child knows that its mother sees something when she looks at it;
it knows of itself as the recipient of smiling affection or angry
irritability; it begins to assume the idea of possession of the toes
she coos over and the sides she tickles. This means that before
the Mirror Stage, a conception of Subject is already present and
based almost entirely on the gaze of the mother upon the baby,
and the hypotheses she forms about it ('*Are you hungry?*'; '*Look
at that grumpy face!*', etc.); but within months, the notion of this
alter ego seen by the baby in its mother's eyes will lay the basis
for the child's own response to its mirror image.

The mother's gaze is the child's first mirror; the child's
identity or notion of itself as a whole being is first formed in that
gaze; it is a narcissistic manoeuvre that underpins the development of identity. This may lead to an interesting reflection upon
the development of the child's identity *if the mother's gaze fails* to
be the baby's first mirror. Studies of institutionalised babies,

made in the mid twentieth century, showed that even when adequately cared for, they failed to thrive: they became listless and depressed and some began to fall behind severely in their cognitive development too. Explained in terms of the formation of Subject, this could be because the baby who spends its Mirror Stage in an institution gets, in the place of the clear pool of the mother's steady and loving gaze (and in the consistency of her hypotheses), the shifting waves and ripples of many different and indifferent carers, and can see no image of itself upon which to found its sense of self. The failure of the Mirror Stage may be catastrophic for the development of the Subject.

In some cases, the mother, even if present, may fail as the child's first mirror. One may think then about the *quality* of the mother's gaze: in most cases, it is filled with love, giving the child a positive reflection of itself. Also, it is consistent: the mother's view of the child is *her particular* view, a view invested with delight, with expectation, with prior knowledge of family history, with fears, and indeed with all the complexity of elements that make a human subject, and this gaze shapes the child's identity. Those hypotheses are the proto-mirror in which the child first develops its notion of wholeness and self. But sometimes, the mother's gaze *is not like this*. She may see the child as a fragment of herself, or as a living creature with which she can't identify; or she may fail to anticipate the child's future development as a mature, talking being, viewing it simply as a parcel of needs and demands. A mother who is severely depressed or mentally ill, or for some reason entirely self-centred, may provide the effect of a distorting mirror or no mirror at all for the child. The distorting mirror may produce a narcissistic line of weakness, a 'faultline' upon which identity is built. Even worse, the child who sees *no* 'alter ego' of itself at all may remain at the fragmented body stage in its imagination for far too long, with damaging long-term effects. Some of the symptoms seen commonly as 'autistic' may be interpreted in the light of some failure to lay the narcissistic foundation stone necessary for the development of the child's sense of Subject at this very early phase.

In severe cases of autism, it appears that the 'I' is not 'precipitated in a primordial form' at the Mirror Stage, and the child does not make the mental leap from the fantasy of a fragmented body to that of the wholeness of its self. As a minimum of two subjects are necessary for any communication to take place, the child's lack of the subjective 'I' makes communication impossible. The lack of eye-to-eye contact observed in autistic children can therefore be seen not as a disturbance of the child's capacity for social interaction (which it is, but this merely describes the symptom without getting any closer to the cause) but as a sign of the absence of Subject. Without a subject to enunciate it, language may be totally absent or will develop almost biologically as a system in which the message is not aimed at the other: the autistic child may be able to speak words, but not to use them in the context of communication.

The Subject in the Mirror Stage

The Lacanian Subject is something that resists definition; psychoanalysis is about elucidating it, bringing it out of the shadows cast by the ego. It may be helpful, in most common usage, to think of it as something like 'identity', which at least bridges the conscious and unconscious realms. It is something with no *objective* existence; it is the sum of the signifiers that represent you, and this is precisely why it is only by the 'talking cure' that the Subject can be arrived at. Lacan's further elaborations upon Subject will be seen later.

In the Mirror Stage, the Subject is the active mind that produces the concept of itself as the other in the mirror; but it cannot know (or recognise) itself. The Subject is thus never what it thinks it is, and the ego is the product of the Subject's imaginary game. The ego helps protect the individual against the threat of incoherence and impotence, and provides a fictitious coherence. The Subject is the symbolic part, unconscious but active, which produces unity, although not wholeness; it thinks itself at the source of everything, but is in reality the product of successive images, of language and its signifiers. The signifiers are not produced by the Subject, they are what constitutes it.

3

In the beginning was the word
Structural linguistics and Lacan

Lacan's view was that the characteristic that sets human beings apart from other animals is language: we are speaking beings (*parlêtre*). If language is what makes us human, then the fundamentals of the human psyche should be found in language. Lacan hypothesised a structural mirroring between what we say and the way we think, and even the way our brain is organised: we think like we speak, we speak as we think. This view can be taken as far as the neuropsychology of language and it is possible that language bears the marks of the neuronal organisation, or conversely that our neurones are organised in a way that reflects the structure of language. Lacan's intuition was that this also applied to the unconscious: the unconscious is structured like a language.

The word itself, 'unconscious', requires definition because many liberties have been taken with it over the century since Freud formulated his psychoanalytical concept of it. Under the influence of other early theorists such as Jung, the word took on shadowy, mystical connotations; under the influence of the more behaviourist model, it assumed the shape of something animal-like and instinctive. Lacan was rather appalled by these deviations from the original Freudian model: 'the unconscious as archaic function ... the metaphysical unconscious of Eduard von Hartmann ... above all the unconscious as instinct – all this has nothing to do with the Freudian unconscious ... nothing at all to do with our experience. I will ask analysts a straight question: *have you ever, for a single moment, the feeling that you are handling the clay of instinct?*[1]

For Lacan, the unconscious is comprised of symbolic elements, and because we are speaking beings for whom language is the main vehicle of representation, its building blocks are words, and its structure is grammatical (an oversimplification which will be refined very shortly). This is why discourse in the setting of an analytical session is the only way of working effectively with it.

The unconscious is what the Subject represses, and by definition is therefore not consciously expressible by the Subject; however, it constantly manifests itself, quite without the Subject's intentions, in dreams, unsuccessful/self-defeating acts, slips of the tongue, and even pathological symptoms. These manifestations were for Lacan 'the discourse of the unconscious': *discourse*, because they always show the structure of language. Lacan found with the patients upon his couch, that even what they thought of as their conscious speech obeyed a hidden structure: that their omissions, denegations, 'forgettings', repetitions, etc. contained the discourse of the unconscious. This observation led him to an intense reflection upon what constitutes the unconscious, the manifestations of which have such a language-like structure. He approached this question using theoretical tools being developed by linguists.

Structural linguistics and the unconscious

In order to understand Lacan's view of language and the unconscious, it is necessary to have some knowledge of the work of the linguist Ferdinand de Saussure, who was a great source of inspiration for Lacan. For Saussure, the fundamental building block of language is the Sign – which was commonly thought of as comprising a word plus its meaning; linguistic expression is achieved by the selection and combination of Signs. Saussure's innovation was to say that the linguistic Sign unites not a name and a thing, but a sound-image and a concept: he spoke not, therefore, of words and meanings, but of signifiers and signifieds.

Why was he not content with 'words' and 'meanings'? For a start, words exist in a spoken and a written form, and they can have many meanings; meanings can be expressed in many ways – in pictures, writing, etc. The object, a needle, can exist without the word 'needle'; the word 'needle' can take a written form or a spoken form and it can be uttered in the absence of the object, to which its link is entirely intellectual; it also has other meanings than that of the slim, pointed metallic object with a hole in one end through which thread is introduced, used in sewing. Saussure was not undertaking to generalise about semiotics; he was concerned with linguistics only and wished to analyse the composition of the linguistic Sign in its *primary* form – the form in which human beings first access it, which is speech, composed of sound-images. Speech pre-dates writing by a long way, both in human history and in child development; writing is secondary to speech. Therefore, it was first of all the formation of signs in *speech* that Saussure was interested in, and he was aware of the psychological nature of this process. He emphasised the immateriality (abstract nature) of the linguistic Sign: thus, the signifier (sound image/acoustic image) is not the *material* sound but the hearer's psychological imprint of the sound, the impression it makes on our senses. Also, the signified (concept) is not the object (the chair in front of you) but *the idea of the object* (any chair – the property of being a chair – of which an example may or may not be before you at the time of speaking).

Signified = concept $\rightarrow$ Signifier = acoustic image

These two elements combine in a relationship called 'signification' to produce the linguistic Sign, which is represented in this Saussurian diagram:

$$\text{Sign} \quad = \quad \frac{\downarrow \text{signified} \uparrow}{\text{signifier}}$$

The horizontal line marking the two elements of the Sign is referred to as 'the bar'; the vertical arrows denote the relationship of signification. For Saussure signifiers and signifieds are like words written on a sheet of paper, with the signifier on one side and its signified on the other; they cannot be separated, and yet they cannot occupy the same place.

In a different context, the philosopher Susanne Langer wrote: 'Symbols [what Saussure would have called Signs] are not proxy for their objects but are *vehicles for the conception of objects* ... In talking *about* things we have conceptions of them, not the things themselves; and *it is the conceptions, not the things, that symbols directly mean.* Behaviour towards conceptions is what words normally evoke; this is the typical process of thinking'.[2]

Lacan must have noticed that Saussure's formulation of signifiers and signifieds corresponded with terms that Freud had already used in his writings, and which were not very satisfactorily rendered in French, where the word 'representation' was being used without any discrimination about what exactly was being represented. The German *Vorstellungen* allowed Freud to distinguish between the 'ideas of things' and the things themselves; Freud's *Vorstellungreprasentanzen* are therefore 'representations of the *ideas of things*' – not 'representations of things'. This corresponds very well with 'signifiers' (the symbolic representations) and their relationship with 'signifieds' (the ideas).

Signifiers and the human psyche

From the very birth of psychoanalysis, the spoken word has had a special importance, being the gateway to the patient's psyche; Freud had already pointed out that emotions (affects) attach themselves not to meanings but to signifiers, although he used the term *vorstellungreprasentanzen* – 'ideational-representatives'. Where Freud linked 'drives' with ideational-representatives, in understanding Lacan, the equivalent could be thought of as the 'emotional load attached to signifiers'. What is important is that it is *signifiers* (and not the signifieds) that bear this load.

As a clinician, Lacan was struck by the extent and frequency of disjunction between words and their intended meanings – how the words uttered by the analysand upon the couch often escaped the intentions of the speaker, and expressed something not consciously intended. The more he heard, the weaker the links between signified and signifier appeared to be; and the greater the connection between signifiers among themselves. Lacan, who liked to use paradox, sought to highlight the primacy of the signifier in the psyche by rewriting Saussure's model of the Sign in the form of a quasi-algebraic sign in which a capital S (representing the *signifier*) is placed over a lower case and italicised *s* (representing the *signified*), these two symbols being separated by a horizontal 'bar'.

$$\frac{S}{s}$$

This suited Lacan's purpose of emphasising how the signified inevitably 'slips beneath' the signifier, resisting our attempts to delimit it. The importance of the bar is that it conveys the idea of the resistance to meaning inherent in language: meaning does not simply appear spontaneously but involves the act of crossing the bar, and it is in this act that signification, or meaning, is produced.

The crossing of the bar

This may be the quintessentially human act: the intellectual exercise that no other animal performs. Dogs respond to verbal commands, and numerous studies have been carried out to try to show that chimpanzees are capable of using language; some have succeeded in training individual chimpanzees to perform linguistic signs in American Sign Language. However, there is no conclusive evidence that the chimpanzees' 'appropriate use' of these signs (signing 'toothbrush' at bedtime) are any more than Pavlovian trained behaviours, accomplished after months of repetition. The human child needs no training, or even teaching: human beings *acquire* language by simply 'crossing the bar' in the relationship between signifier and signified; and once the bar is crossed, the human psyche is in the entrance hall of the Symbolic realm, with all its vast possibilities.

The notion of a *failure* to 'cross the bar' recurs in Lacanian theory at several points – the failure to cross the bar of metaphor, for example, being both an indicator and a cause of psychosis. But the formulation of signifier/signified has another importance for Lacan: it also underlines the *autonomy* of the signifier in relation to the signified, and it is this autonomy that makes signifiers so highly mobile, so easily lent to different associations of substitution and recombination, and indeed so perfect as the building blocks of human thinking, both conscious and unconscious.

It is important here to note that meaning is given by *the association of signifiers in a signifying chain*. The simple association of signifier with signified is far less important, particularly as this link is not permanent and other signifiers can always be substituted. This substitution of signifiers becomes enormously complex when the child crosses the bar of metaphor, as this allows for multiple layers of signifiers to be substituted (as we shall see later on). The same signifieds may therefore be represented by a vast array of different signifier chains; for example, the idea of failure or impotence may lurk beneath the bar of a range of different signifying chains: '*I did not get into Oxford or Cambridge*', '*She was not impressed by what I said*', or '*She manages to live on very little*'… The associations between signifiers and their high mobility allow for the immeasurable complexity of human psychological functioning, both conscious and unconscious.

The making of the unconscious

The newborn, in a world of primary functioning, has no unconscious and a limited consciousness; unlike Freud and many psychologists, however, Lacan did not think that the baby is simply a set of drives and physical needs. For Lacan, the baby, born with the human potential of thinking, does from the very start display a kind of proto-thinking: it forms concepts and hypotheses from its earliest days. Its very first concepts are based upon the dialectic of comfort/discomfort, presence/absence: it recognises a change in environment if mother is there or not, and then, by means of facial recognition, forms an *idea of mother* – a signified, with the glimmer of signifier attached to it, even when the baby is unable to pronounce 'mama'. Other signifieds are formed in a similar fashion, they already have proto-signifiers for the baby, and await the signifiers designated by language to be attached to them. And yet, even before they have become represented by a socially recognised symbolic element, these signifieds already have some power, and can be thought of as unexpressed concepts.

It is this ability to think that makes the pre-language baby able, for instance, to find humour in situations: one has seen a baby laughing uproariously at the sight of a helium-filled balloon bobbing about against the ceiling – the baby has already formed a conception of the law of gravity, which the balloon is disobeying. The proto-conceptualisations of the newborn will be discussed in greater detail later on in the book; for now, what is important is that it is the acquisition of language that allows the human infant the possibility of conceptual representation within the framework of human society, and the possibility of a far greater subtlety and flexibility in the elaboration of abstract ideas.

From the point at which the baby or small child begins to formulate its thoughts in language, there is the possibility of the creation of the unconscious. There comes a moment at which for the first time, a thought occurs which is unbearable to the child; and for the first time, its psychic apparatus represses it. And what does it repress? The signifier with which the thought was formulated.

For Lacan, there are no signifieds in the unconscious, only signifiers. If there were signifieds as well, then the meaning of any particular signifier for a Subject would be quite rigid: a signifier (and its emotional load) would remain immovable, attached forever to one particular thing and not be transferable to another. Fortunately, this is not so, because if it were, then a signifier, once repressed, would be evermore irretrievable. For example, because at a certain moment, the idea of 'loss' may be unbearable to the Subject, the Subject would never be able to use the word 'loss' in conscious speech again. This would be a very rare occurrence and a sign of psychopathology. In fact, what is repressed is usually *a configuration of signifiers* (a signifier in a certain relationship with other signifiers); this means that the signifier itself is still accessible in other contexts. Only in extreme cases is a signifier completely erased – this process is not repression but *foreclosure*.

In the unconscious, signifiers may also come apart into their constituents, sometimes down to individual phonetic elements (the letter-sound). These elements recombine into new signifiers; and perhaps these new signifiers might recombine into new chains. Lacan held that the letter-sound, as the smallest part of a signifier, was the smallest recombinable element; the first letter-sound of a signifier is particularly important, as any child would recognise: a six year old who has just learned to spell his/her name will attach a special significance to the letter with which it begins.

This primary repression creates an aspect of the psyche which is inaccessible to consciousness – the unconscious. Rather than the topological representations used by Freud, one may think of the unconscious as the force field that orientates the molecules of a liquid crystal, where the molecules are the signifiers. The analogy of the liquid crystal is useful when describing the relation of signifiers inside the unconscious: they behave similarly to the molecules in the crystal, forming bonds between themselves, and under the influence of some energy-source, freely slide over one another to form different bonds with other molecules within the crystal. In the unconscious, signifiers develop the same type of relationship between themselves as they do in the conscious psyche: they form themselves into the 'signifying chain'. The unconscious is not within the Subject's control or even view, but it acts in spite of the ego, constantly throwing out signifiers that the Subject has repressed. It is at its most unruly in small children. The elements in the unconscious are the signifiers that represent wishes, desires, fears, and images.

The act of repression may bury the signifier linked with an unpleasant affect (emotion), but it cannot bury the affect. After the signifer is repressed, the now 'orphaned' affect roams free in the psyche, seeking another signifier to which it may attach. This forms the basis of Freud's theory of displacement: the 'roaming' affect may take, for example, the form of a feeling of worry or fear which the child attaches to some other signifier (maybe spiders or baldness), becoming worried about or fearful of a thing which was never the true cause of the fear. The re-attachment process itself is not random but controlled by a signifying chain formed in the unconscious, and this is why it is possible in analysis, to 'source' the re-attachment of the affect to the apparently nonsensical object, by a work of retrieving the repressed signifying chain from the unconscious.

Lacan held that in the signifying chain, any one signifier has meaning through its connection with other signifiers, through its place in the chain. An anorexic girl may say: '*I just want to be thin*', but in her unconscious, *thin* is the end of a long associative chain – *in control, happy like when I was seven, pure and powerful as that child, not with this fat, these blobs, it's embarrassing ...*' It is by bringing into conscious speech the links of this chain that the patient can move further and further towards the core of his/her Subject – for the chain will go on a long way beyond those very few signifiers given in the example.

> The development of a discourse may take place along two different semantic lines: one topic may lead to another through their similarity [metaphoric way] or through their contiguity [metonymic way].[3]

Signifieds derive their coherence from the network of signifiers. The chain of signifiers governs the set of the signified, and words derive their full meaning from their association with others. These associations are performed by means of the two primary processes of selection and combination: when we speak we select a certain number of linguistic units from our mental lexicon and we combine them. These processes are described as the paradigmatic axis (selection) and the syntagmatic axis (combination). The axis of selection concerns the system of language (*langue*) in that it entails lexical choice, while in speech (*parole*), the use of chosen lexical terms depends on the axis of combination. The existence of these two axes can be inferred from the different clinical manifestations of aphasia – a neurological disorder that affects the speech centres.

There are many types of aphasia, of which the two most classic seem to demonstrate the existence of the two axes of linguistic association. The first involves individuals who cannot access words, that is, their ability to select from the lexicon of linguistic signs is affected. If, for instance, they wanted to tell you that your hat was on the chair, they would not be able to find the words '*hat*' or '*chair*', but might be able to convey that '*Your thingy is on the thingy*'. In this kind of aphasia, one might postulate that the paradigmatic axis has been affected. In the other form of aphasia, the individual can access the words but cannot combine them: they would be able to name '*hat*' and '*chair*', but not come out with '*Your hat is on the chair*'; this suggests that the syntagmatic axis is affected.

Metaphor operates along the axis of lexicon (paradigmatic). A metaphor is a figure of speech in which a name or descriptive word or phrase is transferred to an object or action different from, but analogous to, that to which it is literally applicable. Thus, it is a stylistic figure based on relations of similarity. Metaphor consists of referring to something by the name of something else. For example: *a star is born*. This metaphor consists of a linguistic sign, 'star', which consists of the signifier 'star' and a signified, which is the concept of a person who has the properties of brilliance and of high rank. But there is no mention of a person, and the signifier 'star' could anyway have a number of different signifieds, including a celestial body of great mass and energy, or a five-pointed shape. In order for the listener to understand the metaphor, a number of mental operations must be carried out. Firstly, there must be a selection of the correct signified associated with the signifier 'star' and an expulsion of the others. Secondly, the listener must insert the idea of a person beneath the signifying bar of 'star' in order to form a new signified composed of some of the properties of a star added to the idea of a person. However, the idea of a person has to be represented, because meaning arises from the crossing of the bar of signification. This means that the signifier 'person' would also have to have been there, subliminally, before being deleted. In other words, for the metaphor to work, the listener must have mentally inserted an unspoken linguistic sign, 'person', in a process of several stages. This is how it would work:

(Unspoken)   (Spoken)

$\dfrac{\text{S1}}{s1}$ acoustic image of 'person' $\dfrac{\text{S2}}{s2}$ acoustic image of 'star'
   idea of person   idea of brilliance and
                         high rank

(Spoken metaphor)

$\dfrac{\text{S2}}{\dfrac{\text{S1}.s2}{s1}}$ acoustic image of 'star'
          the linguistic sign 'person' is unspoken beneath
          the bar and when the listener crosses it she/he
          links the acoustic image 'star' with a new signi-
          fied resulting from the addition of the ideas of
          brilliance and high rank to the idea of a person:
          $s1 + s2$ makes a new signified, and S1 is deleted.

(Understood metaphor, created by the crossing of the bar)

(deleted) S1 $\leftarrow$ $\dfrac{\text{S2}}{s1 + s2}$ $=$ $\dfrac{\text{S2}}{s3}$ 'star'
                                  idea of brilliant high-ranking
                                  person

The metaphor is now a new sign (let's call it S3) made up of the acoustic image 'star' and a new signified.

This deals, of course, only with the metaphor 'star' in the sentence; there is also 'born', which, for a person unable to understand metaphor, might have rather disturbing connotations; here again, a complex mental operation must be performed. Lacan's point is that the human faculty of complex and abstract thinking is built upon the ability of the mind to perform these feats of substitution, selection, deletion, addition, and the crossing of many bars of signification so effortlessly that one doesn't even think about the mechanics of it; and yet it is worth knowing the mechanics because these very same processes produce the manifestations of our unconscious, and indeed it is *only* by understanding these processes that we ever will understand why we think and feel what we do.

In certain cases of psychosis, the patient finds it impossible to cross the bar in metaphor, or to perform the mental acts of substitution, addition, and deletion. In the above example, *a star is born*, an unwanted signified such as 'idea of a five-pointed shape' might intrude in the mind of a psychotic patient, as might some disturbing image of a live birth. Even outside psychosis, if the words of a metaphor were taken in their literal meaning or out of context, the phrase would probably be considered illogical or funny.

This literality is normal in young children; it is also observed in deaf people who, after having been fitted with a prosthesis, start to hear and learn to speak; difficulty in understanding metaphor is one of the characteristics of some pervasive developmental disorders in children (for example Asperger's disorder).

Metonymy and synecdoche function along the syntagmatic axis of language – by the relationship of contiguity between signifiers. Metonymy is a figure of speech characterised by the action of substituting for a word or phrase denoting an object, action, institution, etc., a word or phrase denoting a property or something associated with it: *Downing Street said, the Crown will prosecute, the pen is mightier than the sword.*

Metonymy: S2 is substituted for S1 but they have to remain in a relation of contiguity. s2 [the idea of a crown] is expelled.

$$\frac{S1 \text{ [signifier of the State]}}{s1 \text{ [signified of the State]}} \quad \star \quad \frac{S2 \text{ [signifier of Crown]}}{s2 \text{ [signified of Crown]}} \quad \rightarrow \quad \frac{S2}{s1}$$

Metonymy is sometimes confused with synecdoche: in synecdoche, the whole is represented by the naming of a part of it, or vice versa: *a day at the wheel, a sail on the horizon, I'll have the lamb.*

A sail on the horizon. The part (a sail) is used for the whole (a ship):

$$\frac{S1}{s1} \quad \text{acoustic image ship/idea of a ship}$$

$$\frac{S2}{s2} \quad \text{acoustic image sail/idea of a sail}$$

Synecdoche: S2 is substituted for S1 but they remain in a relation of contiguity. s2 [the idea of a sail] is expelled. The process of synecdoche formation is the same as metonymic formation; the difference is that in synecdoche, there is a physical relationship between the usual signifieds of the signifier present and the signifier absent, whereas in metonymy, the relationship between the two implied signifieds is not physical but one of possession of properties (an intellectual possesses a pen, where a warrior possesses a sword; 'Downing Street' only works as metonymy while the prime minister lives there: if he moved to Tottenham Court Road, then 'Downing Street' would lose its metonymic meaning).

In metaphor, metonymy, and synecdoche there is a substitution of signifiers; however, the substitution in metaphor is made on the basis of similarity of properties, while in metonymy/synecdoche, the substitution is made on the basis of contiguity of ideas. For example, the phrase *to fish for pearls* uses metonymy, drawing from *fishing* the notion of taking things from the ocean, although fish themselves are not involved. What remains similar is the domain of usage and the associations, but we understand the phrase *in spite of* rather than *because of* the literal meaning of fishing: we know you do not use a fishing rod or net to get pearls. In contrast, the metaphorical phrase *fishing for information* transfers the concept of fishing into an *entirely new domain*, and uses not the contiguity of signifieds but the similarity in the properties of the process itself, which may involve waiting, hoping, tentatively casting about...

The discourse of the unconscious

The hypothesis that the unconscious is structured like a language is based on the Freudian theory of dreams. Dream work involves unconscious mechanisms such as condensation and displacement, which transform latent thoughts into manifest thoughts. The role of these mechanisms is to hide from the dreamer his/her own disturbing unconscious thoughts – or for Lacan, the disturbing signifiers in his/her unconscious; but as the affects that accompany the signifiers cannot be repressed, these are often present and disturbing in dreams.

Condensation involves the process of creating a new 'idea of a thing' by means of joining up other 'ideas of things': for instance, a character in a dream may be a composite of ideas of other characters, or even the idea of a character and the idea of a thing. However, because there are only signifiers in the unconscious, the linkage of the signifiers belonging to these ideas often gives a surreal result.

Displacement is the process in which an affect linked to an idea is detached from it and linked to another one, which has only associative links with the first. For example, the dreamer dreams of a funeral, but rather than feeling sad or upset, experiences a state of joy. Something that is the source of happiness is still hidden from the dreamer, but the affect is displaced onto this other scene, the funeral. Displacement is often what gives to a dream its sense of bizarreness.

One can easily see how Lacan could take these notions of condensation and displacement into his own theory of signification and the unconscious by replacing Freud's ideational-representatives (*vorstellungreprasentanzen*) with 'signifiers'. This allows a new step to be made – that of seeking out the connections inherent in the dream *by means of the structure of language*. According to Lacan, 'the dream has the structure of a sentence … of a rebus … it has the structure of a form of writing [which] reproduces the simultaneously phonetic and symbolic use of signifying elements, which can also be found both in the hieroglyphs of ancient Egypt and in the characters still used in China.'

Lacan suggests that condensation is a metaphoric process and displacement a metonymic one. In language, the substitution of one signifier for another in a metaphor takes place between two terms with a 'traceable' similarity. In dreams this similarity is not always immediately identifiable when it occurs at an unconscious level, but if the analyst working with a patient's dream expects that some of the chains of words used to describe the dream have a metaphoric and a metonymic/synecdochal structure, she/he may help the patient 'chase' the substituted signifier through the patient's associations.

A young woman dreams that she's looking into a big chest full of clothes and strange objects. She finds what looks like the skin of a monkey but realises that it is actually still alive. She experiences a sudden outburst of violence and crushes one of the animal's feet with her bare hands. She can feel the bones cracking.

During the session, this patient described how she '*crushed the monkey's foot*', and tried unsuccessfully to remember a scene in her life in which a monkey or a foot were involved. When asked to go through the description again, she says: '*I can feel his foot being broken in my grip ... the crushing of his toes ... his tootsies*' and suddenly remembers that Tootsie was the childhood nickname of her older sister, with whom she had a relationship of intense rivalry.

In this dream, you can see the process in which her sister, Tootsie, has been disguised as a foot. The similarity is that the foot has toes, which could be called tootsies, and her sister had a nickname that was Tootsie. The initial substitution is metaphorical because there is no connection between her sister and a toe; it has been further disguised by a synecdoche, in that the thing being crushed was the foot of which the toe was a part, and only through an association did the dreamer arrive at the repressed signifier chain – that '*she was crushing Tootsie*'.

Displacement in dreams can be seen as a metonymic process: the essential part of the latent material appears secondary at a manifest level; it is represented by the incidental. The relation of contiguity can be revealed only by associations, as in the following example.

A young woman has talked to her analyst for some time about her difficult relationship with her parents: her mother is severely obsessional and her father used his daughter as a confidant, telling her in particular inappropriate details about his sexual life. She left home as soon as she could and has avoided contact with her parents for many years. This is a dream she told during a session three days after a holiday during which she saw her father but failed to talk to him:

> *There was this man who wanted to kill me. I knew it. I was hiding behind a bush with two children, a boy and a girl ... trying to protect them. I went to hide in a building. It was a library. People were lying on the floor – lots of people, like as if they were sleeping. I tried to hide in the middle of them, I wanted to melt within all the bodies. The children were gone. The man went into the library and without difficulty he found me. I was not scared even though I knew he wanted to kill me. So I stood up and stabbed him with a pen. I felt the pen entering his chest and there was blood everywhere. He was in pain and the situation looked terrible but I felt relieved. The people around me did not react at all, as if all this was normal – expected.*

The contiguity of the signifiers that she uses reveals the meaning of this dream: she hides in a library (she has hidden from her problems in books for much of her life), but this does not stop the man from threatening her. She tries to hide amongst bodies (she had in reality a promiscuous past in which her many, indiscriminate sexual contacts were a way of 'losing' herself in other bodies); she stabs him with a pen (in real life, she did not want to talk to her father; however, she had written a letter to him, to vent some of her anger – she wanted to hurt him, with her pen). The man is now in pain, and 'the situation looked terrible', but she experiences some relief from her act (as she did from writing the letter). And finally, the act which sounds so extreme, creates no shock in anyone else: it seems that it's actually something that could be considered 'normal – expected' – as unremarkable, in fact, as the sending of a letter. In this dream, the patient's narrative is almost exactly a narrative of how she has dealt with the emotional problems posed by her father, and her recent real-life experience, but omits all the key signifiers and substitutes them with others, so that it is only in the *contiguity of the signifiers* that the meaning resounds.

In the unconscious, not only signifiers may be substituted or combined in hidden associations, but their component parts may be too. For Lacan, signifiers could be broken down into smaller phonic elements, and sometimes, a single letter-sound may carry a message. At others, phonemes from a repressed signifier may recombine to produce a new signifier, as in the following dream, recounted by a Jewish woman living in London.

> *There was this really annoying spider – I am afraid of spiders, but this one was more annoying than scary. It just kept bothering me, and somehow, I had to be nice to it. I couldn't just squash it, I had to talk to it. But it kept getting in my face and annoying me. It looked, well, not much like a spider – more a little ball of fluff with a dark centre and sort of light woolly hair coming off it.*

In talking about it, she realises that the feelings she has articulated towards this spider are the same feelings she has been experiencing towards a neighbour, whom she suspects of having an affair with her husband. She has described this neighbour as 'lightweight', 'an airhead', and racist – in a previous session, she said that this woman would have, during World War II, been a Nazi sympathiser. Her description of the spider describes her annoyance with the woman, 'a bit of fluff' to whom she is obliged to be 'nice', even though she hates her and fears her. One can imagine that the signifier *Nazi 'sympathiser'* – how she thinks of the neighbour – could be reduced to the phonic elements 's' – 'p' – 'i' – 'er' and recombined into 'spider' – and the fact that this dream is *not* about a spider is confirmed in the un-spider-likeness of the description of a lightweight ball of blond-ish fluff.

It is not only in dreams that unconscious speech appears: it appears also in slips of the tongue, in accounts of self-defeating acts, in denegation (saying the opposite of what you unconsciously mean), in grammatical errors, in people's choice of subject matter when they speak, and in countless other ways. Slips of the tongue may also be slips of the pen, or the keyboard, where again, a simple typographical error may be revealing.

The mother of an anorexic girl, who was a very controlling woman, had great problems in accepting the relationship between her daughter and the psychiatrist, which is one that necessarily excluded her. This mother wrote a letter to the psychiatrist in which she sought to influence the way in which the psychiatrist thought, telling him in some detail her understanding and interpretation of her daughter's behaviour and emotional state. Her aggression was restrained within socially acceptable bounds up until the end of the text, which concluded: '*You see, that's how the anorexic minx works.*' She had probably intended 'mind'.

Many of the symptoms encountered in psychopathology also follow this linguistic structure and can be seen as metaphors. This time, it's not a dream image that is linked to a metaphoric process but the symptom itself. For example, a teenage boy has started to regularly pass out at school; he passes out only at school, never at home, and all medical tests have revealed that there is no organic cause for his losses of consciousness. During sessions, he starts to talk about the fact that he has become quite 'naughty' (rebellious, sexually interested) and he's afraid that his mum is going to suffer because of that. He's also scared that his father, who travels a lot and is rarely at home, will be very cross when he comes back. Talking about the episodes of losses of consciousness, he says, 'When I pass out, I can't do anything at school,' and realises that the symptom is for him a way of *not doing anything* [*naughty*] at school.

The analyst may use the metaphoric (or metonymic) structure of the patient's own discourse to try to help unveil the signifier. A ten-year-old boy developed an irrational fear of vomiting, which was not linked with any digestive illness. He was old enough to know that it was irrational, and tried to hide it from his parents, who were going through a divorce. This fear began to overwhelm him: he could not concentrate at school, was miserable at home, and spent his time making sure he was near a toilet in case he had to throw up. When his parents finally discovered his strange fear, he was sent to a therapist. He said: '*I don't know why I think I'll throw up. It's just that sometimes, it's like there's something stuck in my throat ... I feel sick, and I can't swallow it.*' The therapist knew his parents were splitting up – a fact that was very hard for the boy to accept, that 'sticks in the craw': he entered into this metaphorical structure and asked: '*What is it that's so hard for you to swallow?*' – opening the door for the boy's unconscious knowledge of the cause of his anxiety to be represented in speech.

The symptom may operate at more than one level of anxiety and almost always does. Before reaching the point of realisation that his parents' divorce may be at the centre of his anxieties, the boy had also said of his strange behaviour: '*I have to be near the toilet because if I throw up, I'll get myself dirty ... I'll soil myself.*' It transpired that the boy, who was in many ways a model child, had once had an embarrassing episode of soiling himself when he was four, which caused him great shame and stress and had provoked in him a fear that his parents would despise him and not love him any more. To him, the signifier 'soiling' was intimately linked with the signifiers which signified loss of parental love: his parents' imminent separation might have indicated a loss of love for him as well, and could have been seen as being 'his fault' if he got himself dirty.

The passage between the conscious and unconscious mind of signifiers is constant and banal. It is not only in analysis that a repressed signifier reappears: it may spontaneously do so without any help from someone else, in the absence of the need to repress it any longer; equally, repression may be occasional, temporary, and trivial – it may cause you to 'forget' someone's name for the ten minutes in which you needed it.

Lacan placed much emphasis on signifiers, but it is important to understand that signifiers are essentially symbolic elements, which in special circumstances may take another form than speech. Deaf people, for example, use unspoken signifiers, but the same rules (adapted to the visual) would apply for them. An interesting and productive line of reflection for a clinician is upon the particularities or perhaps even the complete absence of the unconscious in severely autistic children who have never developed any language.

The master signifiers

These are the very backbone of the human Subject; they are also, perhaps in negative form (in the sense of the negative of a photograph), the stuff of denegation. A listener with a trained ear will be able, over the course of a relatively short period of time, to recognise the master signifiers of a speaker. They appear in those declarations that make, when examined, no logical sense to the listener (because they obey a logic entirely personal to the speaker). They are often repeated, in different contexts, sometimes so much that they come to constitute a linguistic tic in the speaker, for whom they have a significance that is nothing to do with the literal signified of the signifiers (this is not to be confused, however, with that common feature in the speech of children, who upon learning a new word or a new bit of playground slang, use it *ad nauseam*). Before I explain exactly what a master signifier is, consider the following example.

An eleven-year-old girl had been bullying another in her class; the teachers were concerned that her behaviour was linked with the death, the previous year, of her father. After a few sessions, the psychologist noticed that she used the word 'lucky' a lot, often in ways that made little sense or in contexts that were fairly uninteresting or inappropriate. '*I'm so lucky, because I haven't got to go to the hairdressers*' or '*There were five purple bracelets and four pink ones, and I'm so lucky, I got one of the purple ones*' – indeed, 'I'm so lucky' was so over-used that one had to consider the meaning of it. The girl's bullying was of another girl who had been put down for a private school that she (the Subject) had wanted to go to, but which was too expensive for her family. When asked obliquely about this – the school was merely mentioned – she said: '*I'm so lucky, you know why? I haven't got to take the entrance exam!*'

One can see how the function of 'I'm so lucky' is to orientate the other signifiers in the signifying chain into a fiction that supports her ego. If you took the 'I'm so lucky' out of the sentence about the school, she would be left with '*I haven't got to take the entrance exams*' – which might point up too plainly the painful truth that she wasn't put down for the school in the first place. 'I'm so lucky' is the 'spin' she puts on it, and 'spin', even if rather too fashionable a term, is not a bad word in this context, for it describes exactly what Lacan said that master signifiers do: orientate and give direction.

A woman in her early fifties complained endlessly about the behaviour of her young adult sons. '*They're really too much!*' was her constant refrain, and was applied to descriptions of almost every action of theirs – bringing a girlfriend to the family's holiday home, having a few friends around for a week in the summer – things many listeners might not consider unreasonable.

It appears that she was always called upon to cater for the needs of the guests as well as her family, and resented this. Friends had advised her that if she didn't want to, she shouldn't do it, but she never felt that she could stop; nor did she feel that she could enunciate her resentment to her family in any direct way. In the 'too much'-ness of her complaints about those close to her (her husband got much the same portrayal) could be heard her own sense of being 'too little' appreciated; it is no surprise to discover that she had had this feeling of insignificance in comparison with her siblings from her earliest memories. The truth of her Subject was that she was the one who didn't matter, who never felt adequately loved, and who was constantly overlooked. 'Littleness' or insignificance, rather than 'too much'-ness was her master signifier, in contrast to what she could pronounce.

The master signifiers usually mask their opposites, or perhaps one should say they exist in a polarised form, with the audible side propping up the ego and the unenunciated buried in the unconscious, but constantly pushing up at its opposite number. Their function is to redirect signifiers in a signifying chain painful to the speaker in such a way that a signifying chain with the opposite, bearable, or even comforting meaning emerges in conscious speech. They are not new inventions of the speaker; they have been laid down at some quite early point in the Subject's life, although they may assume different guises to suit the linguistic fashions of the day. In the case of the eleven-year-old girl, 'lucky' was laid down as a master signifier many years before the death of her father. She had always defended herself against problems of jealousy of her older brother (and later friends at school) by insisting upon the 'luck' she had in life – 'I'm so lucky, I won the pass-the-parcel!' etc. – and inserting it in many situations in which to most people the luck factor would seem irrelevant. In fact, the true master signifier was the exact opposite – 'lucky' was the mask behind which was hiding 'unlucky' and her deep sense of (imagined) injustice and anxiety that other people had it better than her. Upon the death of her father, the sudden increase in genuine bad luck in her life was greeted with a massive effort on her part to maintain her fiction with the use of her master signifiers; and there they were – already in place in the vanguard of her ego, ready to raise their shields when required.

The master signifiers are those that, for the Subject, have become quite detached from their signifieds, but carry out the function of changing the meaning of the signifying chain into one that supports the ego. It is one of the main tasks of analysis to unmask these master signifiers, and to bring to light the side of them that is hidden in the unconscious. This may sound like a terrifying prospect for the ego, but Lacan never said that the ego had to be demolished for the Subject to be revealed. Rather, he used a metaphor in which the ego was an edifice built around master signifiers in whose shadow their negative counterparts are obscured. Analysis is therefore more like the movement of the sun that brings these negatives into the light: the ego can remain intact, but now we can see the whole thing more clearly.

One of the more difficult points that Lacan made about the master signifier was to equate it with the Name-of-the-Father. This is not as mystical as it seems, but in order to understand it, one must first understand what he means by the Name-of-the-Father, the Phallus, the *objet petit a* (chapters 6 and 7), and also his ideas about the place of desire in the construction of the Subject and its ego. I hope that this equation of the Name-of-the-Father with the master signifiers will become quite obvious to readers by the end of this book.

4

The Other

Lacan's linguistic hypotheses concern the kind of speech an analyst listens for in a patient; he is not a linguist making a general theory of language. The manifestations (or discourse) of the unconscious – dreams, slips of the tongue, pathological symptoms, etc. – are always signifiers in a signifying chain that seems to 'happen' to the Subject as if sent from somewhere else. Lacan held that the analysand's ego mistakes this unconscious discourse for a discourse that comes from the Other.

The 'other' and the 'Other'

The concept of 'otherness' is central to Lacanian thinking. He constantly posits the Subject as coming into being by means of its relationship with otherness, an insight inspired by his interest in Hegelian dialectics, which described the formation of self-consciousness as the result of a struggle between entities. For Lacan, 'otherness' took two forms: in 1955, he made a distinction between *le petit autre* (small other) and *le grand autre* (*Autre* or Other with a capitalised first letter). *Le petit autre* derives from the Mirror Stage: it is not a real 'other' but the reflection and projection of the ego. As such, it belongs in the realm of the Imaginary; it also gives rise later to the concept of *l'objet petit a* (the small a object), which is dealt with in chapter 8. Apart from the small other in the mirror, the individual comes to recognise all other people as 'little others', and to treat them as suitable objects of projection and identification. On the other hand, *le grand autre* – the Other – indicates a radical otherness which is beyond the Imaginary and which cannot be resolved and dealt with through identification. This otherness comes from language and the Law – *le grand autre* belongs to the Symbolic order.

At the beginning of his teaching, Lacan uses the letter *a* (in lower case) to represent the small other (object of the self or *petit autre*) constituted in the Mirror Stage. It is used to distinguish the imaginary dimension within which the self constitutes its ego from the symbolic big Other (represented by a capital *A* for *l'Autre*). The Other is Society, the Law, etc. – the whole set of hypotheses within which the Subject is constituted – it is an illustration of the fact that the Subject is part of an order which predates its birth and is exterior to the self. This order is symbolic, and because its most elaborate and influential manifestation is language, the Other is sometimes used to designate language itself.

Language as the Other

Language pre-existed the child, and the child's parents; it is a lexicon of words and a rulebook handed down over the millennia. It was created by humankind and is the primary form in which the human subject experiences the human-ness of Society. The psychoanalyst, listening to the speech of the Subject upon the couch, hears this Other discourse. It is not a discourse that the Subject intends, but that it cannot help but produce; it is obvious in the unintended emergence of repressed signifiers, be they in slips of the tongue, in dreams, or in pathological symptoms. Lacan held that the analysand's ego mistakes this unconscious discourse for a discourse that comes from the Other. It also returns to the Subject in the words uttered by the analyst when she/he makes an interpretation: the discourse of the analyst is experienced by the Subject as the discourse of the

Other – the great treasury of knowledge, rules, and hypotheses that constitutes the Symbolic realm.

Many people picture the unconscious as a 'hidden character' inside the individual's mind, or, as Freud drew it, an area in the psyche. Lacan's view is radically different: as seen in the previous chapter, the signifiers repressed into the unconscious continue to exist, despite the Subject's antipathy towards them, because of the Other, the lexicon to which they belong, and they emerge from time to time in a form and structure dictated by this Other. The unconscious therefore exists within an abstract matrix – the discourse of the Other – and like the electromagnetic field operating upon a liquid crystal to form letters, it pulls signifiers into place in this matrix.

The Subject is constituted from the Other

The Lacanian Subject also exists in the discourse of the Other: it is created even before the baby is born in the discourse of its parents, a little like a registered 'domain name' on the Internet – a marker where a website may one day come into being. The parents talk about the child, or at least have in their minds some ideas and fantasies about the child, even before it is born. These ideas – this discourse – is formulated by their own Subjects and unconsciousness within the Other, which is the set of hypotheses into which they, too, were born. And in speaking of their hopes and fears, these parents are to some extent already 'giving birth' to the new Subject. If one takes this idea further, the Subject could exist whether or not the person is alive. This is not just a philosophical fancy: it has clinical relevance, as one may see how a dead child or a past patriarch may still act like a Subject within the dynamics of a family.

At the start of its life, the Other for the child is embodied by the mother, who is for this reason in some contexts synonymous with the Other; it is from this Other that the child acquires language, as well as the set of laws and hypotheses to which she subscribes. This transmission of the Other from mother to child is, for Lacan, the primary identification (remember that identification is the process whereby the Subject assumes the *underlying structure* of another, so that its development, whatever the environmental circumstances, is governed by that structure). In Lacan's words, 'primary identification ... occurs on the basis of the mother's omnipotence [and] makes the satisfaction of needs dependent upon the signifying apparatus, [which] also fragments, filters and models those needs in the defiles of the signifier's structure'.[1] In other words, in acquiring speech from the mother, the child acquires also the mother's attitudes, rules, and assumptions – indeed, the whole Other of the mother.

The infant acquires language by hearing its parents speak; and as it 'crosses the bar' of meaning and begins to apply signifiers to its object self (the small other it recognised in the mirror), it seeks in everything it hears – particularly in the discourse of its parents – clues for the development of its ego. The Subject becomes subsumed into the fiction built by the parents' discourse, which is readily absorbed into the child's ego. For instance, if the parents' discourse is that '*Sally doesn't really like dolls, she much prefers running around in the garden*', this may become one of the founding myths of Sally's view of herself (her ego): she is not the kind of girl who likes dolls, she is sporty, a tomboy. In its search for identity the child is profoundly narcissistic; its mental response to everything that's said is necessarily: *What is my part in this? How does this relate to me?* So: the parents talk about football; the child thinks: *They are interested in football – if I play football, they'll be interested in me.* The parents talk about some celebrity's recent makeover; the child thinks: *They admire this celebrity – am I like her in some way?* The parents talk about their university days, and the child notes instantly that it is from a family of graduates and expects a similar future for itself. Thus is the Subject developed *in the discourse of the Other*. However, this discourse, consisting of signifiers, allows also for repression: for every element inserted into the edifice of the ego, which is the fiction the Subject loves, there is another that is repressed into the unconscious.

The Subject is revealed in the Other

For Lacan, the Subject remained that elusive thing that hides behind the ego, that is alienated from it, that is created in an act of language, and that is largely unconscious. It is the Subject that speaks; but when it speaks, it barely knows what it is saying. And I am no longer referring here to the 'unconscious discourse' that appears in slips of the tongue, dreams, and pathological symptoms, I am referring to what the speaker (Subject) would think of as 'conscious speech'. This is because for the most part, the Subject is unconscious of itself.

This view may seem like overstatement: one feels provoked to say, '*But I do know what I'm talking about ... I only make a slip of the tongue very rarely, 99% of the time I mean exactly what I'm saying*', etc. But the experienced analyst knows instantly when she/he hears denegation ('*Of course, he's likeable enough*' nearly always means I don't like him); and even the most common, everyday use of language is closely governed by the unconscious. Most of the time, there is an interplay of conscious and unconscious in our speech: we may mean exactly what we say, but we hardly ever know why we say it. Consider the following examples:

'*Has so-and-so got a partner?*' appears a simple question, but what motivates it? Is the questioner a woman worried that the so-and-so in question is interested in her man? Or is it a man interested in so-and-so? Or is it a woman who, motivated by jealousy, hopes to learn that so-and-so is unlucky in love where she herself is not? Whichever it is, the speaker is bound to deny it, and say it's an innocent question motivated by altruistic concern or curiosity. And even if that were true, then why the altruism/curiosity? We can never escape the unconscious – even when it is harmless.

'*We've cooked a roast for you – we got the joint from such-and-such specialist butcher*' could provoke guilt in a prodigal child, or encourage a guest to bring a bottle of better quality wine than usual (why not just 'a roast'? Why mention the quality of it?), etc. But again, in both cases, the speaker's intentions are entirely unconscious.

'*I'm still recovering from the weekend*' is a commonly heard phrase, but why does the speaker think the listener needs to know this? Is she/he boasting about her/his exciting social life, bolstering the edifice of an ego which includes the master signifiers 'socially successful' or 'popular'? Or is she/he trying to convince her/himself that she/he had a good time, when in fact she/he was very bored?

Even '*Please may I have a kilo of potatoes*' could be a multi-layered statement: why not simply, 'a kilo of potatoes' – why the time spent on a formula of *politesse*? Is the questioner trying to show her/his good breeding? Or if, on the contrary, all *politesse* is dispensed with – then why the rudeness? Might *that* be a way of establishing higher status over the lowly greengrocer? And is a kilo enough – or is the speaker being mean and not buying enough, or displaying an anxiety about inadequacy and asking for too many?

These trivial examples only underline the power of the unconscious in directing the selection and combination of signifiers into chains with or without our conscious 'will'; Lacan saw this interplay between conscious and unconscious in the Subject as being like the continuum of the surface of a moebius strip.

The Other is manifest not only in language (even though this may be its principal domain), but also in the whole set of hypotheses that exert their influence upon the Subject. The Law, societal rules, taboos, mores and expectations, and even Time are different faces of the Other. The Other is constituted by the entire symbolic realm of human productions; accessing the Other involves the crossing of the bar described in chapter 3; it also involves the act of alienation described in the Mirror Stage, which situates the Subject within the Other. These processes of alienation and symbolisation which tie together Subject and Other are the essential basis of human creativity.

How the Subject gains access to the Other

Access to the Other can be said to happen as a gradual process in which there are also two quantum leaps, or two initiatory 'gateways' through which the child must pass. The first is the Mirror Stage, in which the child is alienated from itself by its identification with its mirror image – a false object onto which it can transfer all the signifiers with which it builds the fiction of its ego. The dialectic created by the dualities of Subject and ego allows the formation of the concepts that can and do attract symbolisation. The 'small other' perceived in the Mirror Stage is the 'idea of self' to which signifiers may attach. A child who has never undergone the alienation of the Mirror Stage may remain locked out of language forever: it has no access to the Other. This would be observable in cases of severe autism. A child for whom the Mirror Stage happens a little late (missing the window of opportunity of usual language development) may need specialist help in overcoming this delay, unlike most children, who develop language with complete ease and naturalness.

The second initiatory gateway is that of castration, which will be dealt with in the next chapter. Briefly here, a failure of this stage would lead not to a total inability to access language but to a psychotic structure in which signifiers do not have the usual autonomy and flexibility of recombination, and the Other (Law, Society, language, and all other symbolic creations) is perceived as having a frighteningly direct relationship with the Subject. Lacan called this relationship with the Other a 'failure to access the metaphor', underlining how essential it is for the psyche to be able to make the complex substitutions of signifiers typified by metaphor in order to comprehend the Other.

Children with language difficulties because of a delay in or problem with building the foundation of the Symbolic (access to the Other) may be particularly resistant to rules and boundaries, because they are locked in an enjoyment of the Imaginary; but even when the foundation is laid normally, a child may still resist other manifestations of the Other. A child who has developed speech at the right time may be uninterested in symbolisation in another form – for example reading, paying attention to time, or even playing games that involve rules – but this behaviour is neurotic rather than psychotic in structure, and indicates a rebellion against the Other rather than a structural weakness that prevents the child from accessing it.

A child has difficulties learning to read, despite encouragement and support from his mother. In a session, he tells the psychiatrist that Mother knows all the words in the world; he knows a few, but she has all of them, in a big book. He doesn't really need to learn to read; it's better if Mum remains the keeper of the Book – she's the grown up, after all.

This description from the child sounds remarkably close to Lacan's own formulation: that the Other is the place where all signifiers are stored – a 'treasury' of words like gold coins in a trunk. In this case, it is not that the child cannot access the treasury, he simply prefers that his mother should remain its keeper: it prolongs a pleasant state of dependency upon Mother and ensures her continued presence.

The Other is omnipresent: all our lives we will play with, struggle against, and learn to use its manifestations. Verbal jokes are directed at the Other – they seek to subvert the Other by slyly playing with the boundaries of obscenity, social acceptability, or with the rules of language itself. A person who bumps against a piece of furniture and automatically says, 'sorry' is addressing the Other; a person who is habitually late may be rebelling against the Other in its guise as Time; the Other is in money: the miser and the gambler are both trying to bend it to their will. But in psychoanalysis, it is the Other as language that is the most important, because of the structuring effect that language has upon the development of the Subject, and because the truth of the Subject can only be apprehended by means of it.

5
The paternal metaphor
The role of the father in the unconscious

> The function of the father in the Oedipus complex is to be a signifier substituted for ... the first signifier introduced in symbolisation, the maternal signifier.
>
> (Lacan, 1958[1])

Primary concepts, primary signifiers

What is the maternal signifier? The very first concept that the newborn baby forms is that of the mother: she exists as a signified even before the baby is able to articulate anything more complex than a cry. The concept of 'Mother' is the baby's first mental act of symbolisation; this concept comprises comfort symbolised in the ideation of a person.

But Mother is not always there. Faced with her absence, the baby performs its first act of repression: the maternal signifier is thus the first signifier that is repressed. Upon her return, the signifier is retrieved: and thus is formed the baby's leaky new unconscious. From the one signifier, with which the baby has such a passionate relationship, arise many concepts – comfort, loss, regaining ... and the beginnings of many hypotheses. The first hypothesis, well known in developmental psychology, is that of the permanence of objects: via the mother's disappear-ances and reappearances, the baby comes to understand that objects persist even when not within its view. But this creates further questions: '*Where is she when she's not with me? Why does she go away?*' These questions are there in proto-conceptual form even in pre-language infants. The 'obvious' answer arrives in the form of the father.

Long before the baby can understand concepts such as 'work' or 'chores' or the myriad other reasons for Mother's absence, it can understand *and see* the reality of Father. He is the other thing in the baby's world which might account for Mother's going away – and proof of it comes when she says to the child: '*It's time to sleep. Mummy and Daddy must have their dinner now.*' Father occupies a place in the child's world as the single biggest distrac-tion for Mummy and therefore the single greatest rival to itself. As the central object in this drama, the mother names the father as the one with whom the baby was made and with whom she also wants to be. These are themes of great power for the child and form the basis for the construction of many infant hypotheses.

The hypothesis made by the child to explain Mother's 'choice' of Father is necessarily that '*Father has something I haven't got.*' But equally, sometimes Mother is with the baby, who might then quite naturally think '*Whatever it is, maybe I have it too.*' The baby has now hypothesised the existence of '*the thing that satisfies Mother*', or in Lacanian terms: the object of Mother's desire. '*What does she want? I'd like it to be me that she wants, but it is clear that it's not just me there is something else on her mind*' (Lacan, 1958[2]).

The Lacanian Phallus

The idea (signified) of the object of the mother's desire is an object that can fill 'the lack in the other'. Lacan named that object the Phallus. The word denotes its imaginary quality: a phallus is never a 'penis' but a representation or image of potency; in mythology, ancient religion, and art, the phallus is always a symbolic object. A feminist interlocutor once suggested that 'uterus' might be a better word for the symbolisation of power – after all, she said, the power of the uterus is real. However, that is precisely the problem with this word: a uterus is a real object, invested with a real and specific power – the power of generation. The whole point of the word *phallus* is that it refers to an entirely imaginary object invested with an *entirely imaginary and undefined* power: it is the imaginary-ness that is important. There is an historical and mythical resonance to it – human tradition created the phallus to express a notion of potency. Also, as we shall see in chapter 9, the castration that is allowed by this representation is one that affects boys more radically than girls. Lacan appropriated the word to denote the imaginary object-of-power that the infant hypothesises *draws Mother away*, or that *perhaps I have, which brings her back*: it is an imagined perfect object.

When the mother is away physically or not paying enough attention to the child, the child may assume that its mother is involved with the object of her desire. Among the hypothetical questions the child forms may be: '*Is that involvement licit?*' and '*Should I accept it?*' How the child eventually answers these questions will be important in determining many facets of its personality structure.

The construction of the paternal metaphor

The object of the mother's desire can be represented by the following sign:

$$\frac{S1}{s1} \quad \text{or} \quad \frac{\text{signifier of the object of mother's desire}}{\text{signified (idea) of the object of mother's desire (Phallus)}}$$

The father can be represented by the following sign:

$$\frac{S2}{s2} \quad \text{or} \quad \frac{\text{signifier of the father}}{\text{idea of the father}}$$

When the mother explains her absence, she does so by means of a metaphor in which she 'blames' it on her submission to rules (Law) and not as an effect of her desire: all her excuses are metaphors, from the infant's point of view – '*It's time to sleep – Mummy and Daddy must have their dinner now ...*' or '*I have to go, Mummy must go to work ...*' To the child, 'must have their dinner now' or 'work' is an excuse veiling an incontrovertible truth: '*Mummy is seeking some other source of satisfaction than me, i.e. the Phallus.*' It must be pointed out that at this stage, the Phallus exists as an idea – a signified – but one to which no definite signifier has been firmly attached: the child is still groping around for what that might be; however, it is represented *enough* to be fitted into a signifier chain such as '*She's gone for thingama-jig again.*' And of all the thingamajigs that could sit most firmly and plausibly above the Phallus, 'Daddy' is by far the most understandable and powerful for the child. Lacan wrote the paternal metaphor thus:

$$\frac{\text{S of the object of mother's desire}}{s \text{ of the object of mother's desire}} \times \frac{\text{S of the father}}{s \text{ of the father}} \rightarrow \frac{\text{S of the father}}{\dfrac{\text{S the object of m's desire}}{s \text{ the object of m's desire (Phallus)}}}$$

The signified associated with the father has disappeared in this metaphorical process and the sign *signifier of the mother's desire/Phallus* becomes the new signified for the signifier of the father. But this has already been symbolised as the Phallus (by 'symbolised' I mean that the child can fit it into a signifier chain – which implies it must have a representation, although this representation is not fixed), so in the substitution process, we get this:

$$\frac{\text{Name-of-the-father}}{\text{desire of the mother}} \times \frac{\text{desire of the mother}}{\text{signified to the Subject}} \rightarrow \frac{\text{Name-of-the-father (O)}}{\text{Phallus}}$$

Lacan calls this metaphor the Name-of-the-Father (sometimes referred to as the 'paternal metaphor'), and as you see, the Name-of-the-Father comes to represent the Other where previously there was only her mysterious desire. 'The Name-of-the-father designates the recognition of a symbolic function defined in the place from which the law exercises its influence.'[3]

In the paternal metaphor, the signifier Father is substituted for the signifier 'object of Mother's desire'. In the course of the substitution the signifier 'object of Mother's desire' is repressed and becomes unconscious; this is part of Freud's 'primal repression' that makes up the kernel of the unconscious (as distinct from secondary repressions in which the already-developed psyche represses thoughts that are unacceptable to it). The signified of the desire of the mother (Phallus) is now associated with the Name-of-the-Father, in a metaphoric structure.

By naming the father as the cause of her absence from the child, the mother is nominating him in a symbolic act of language in the place of the fundamental object of her desire (Phallus) that the child imagines she is after. Both of them know that the reality is not this simple, but the mother must provide an explanation in her speech, and the infant can accept it or not: it is by an act of language that the child's unspoken hypotheses are addressed. Moreover, not only does the mother invoke the Name-of-the-Father in her explanation, the father's very existence in their lives implies the functioning of mother and child within a wider social sphere governed by social rules (the existence of kinship groups, peer relations, etc.). The mother usually reinforces this idea of the wider social realm to explain her absence or preoccupation by couching her excuse in terms suggesting obligation: 'I *have* to go now', 'I *must* have dinner with Daddy', 'I *have* to go to work', etc. She rarely says 'I *want* to go.' In using this formula of obligation, she lets the child know that there are rules and laws 'out there' to which she too must submit: she is *not* the Other, the Other is out there. By accepting the mother's explanation, the child then enters into the game of discourse, and into the Symbolic realm.

With this process the dyadic relationship (involving only two entities) between mother and child becomes triangular – there is a third party, as represented by the father, although it may not be an actual father. The formulation *Name-of-*the-Father is particularly useful here as it emphasises the representative nature of this third party. Lacan points out that Freud himself had tried, in his work, to indicate that the 'father' he wrote about was not meant to be a real father but a representation, except that Freud had called it 'the *dead* Father'. In extracting the symbolic nature of it, the Name-of-the-Father, Lacan makes it clear that this could be a dead or estranged father, or whatever takes the place of Mother's main other role in life (her own family, her work, etc.). However, 'work' is a very much more abstract thing and harder for an infant to imagine than a solid human being, and does not have the mystical quality necessarily attached to a being who has contributed to one's very existence.

Castration and the symbolic realm

There are two important stages, which have different but related effects, in the child's submission to the paternal metaphor:

* The child must form the hypothesis of the Phallus as a reason for Mother's disappearances, a hypothesis which in itself implies a recognition that the mother is not the Other.
* The child must accept the Name-of-the-Father as the repre- sentative possessor of the Phallus; this implies that the child

accepts that it hasn't got it – a symbolic loss described as castration. Castration is the acceptance that one is less-than-perfect, limited, not all-powerful and able to control or satisfy the world. Castration is therefore a symbolic process which allows the child to situate itself within the Law, and to accept that its own desires are not paramount.

Why does submission to the Name-of-the-Father allow the child to situate itself within the Law? The mother is the first representation of the Other to the child, and therefore at the outset, the child's relationship with the Other is a dyadic one. While in this state, the child believes that it is omnipotent, through its identification with its mother, who represents the Other; there is a lack of distinction, therefore, about who makes the Law, who has all the hypotheses, etc. This is also potentially a terrifying state for the child, who is subject to the total power of this mother-Other and might experience her actions as persecutory when she goes away or refuses it something, because it cannot imagine that this Other, being all-powerful, could be acting in accordance with the requirements of a third-party Other, which it has not yet hypothesised. These fantasies of omnipotence or persecution are characteristic of psychosis. The hypothesis of mother's less-than-omnipotence – that she 'needs' something (the Phallus) and that this is what causes her absences or disobedience to the child – is the first step in allowing the child a way out of this condition. The second is that if mother is not perfect and complete and is actually obeying the dictates of 'something or someone else' – a third party – then she is not after all the Other: the Other is this third party. This situation of the Other in a third party outside the dyadic relationship is experienced both as a loss of power for the child (which may still hope to control the mother) and also as a great comfort – for it explains the mother's otherwise frightening behaviour, which previously appeared whimsical and persecutory. Imagine how much less terrifying for the child to be able to think '*She's refusing me this* because *of something*', rather than simply '*She's refusing me*' – a psychological dead-end in which there is no reason why and which generates a feeling of senseless persecution. Thus, the Other becomes more remote, less directly manipulable, but less terrifying, and the child recognises the truth of the matter: the Other is 'out there' in the wider world, which the child is now more inclined to engage with.

Why does access to the paternal metaphor also allow the child to avoid the rigid literality seen in the psychotic structure? The Symbolic is comprised of signifiers and other representations of ideas; signifiers are perhaps the most agile and useful of all, being infinitely flexible in different combinations. All of human intellectual activity, social interaction, and indeed even the formation of the Subject itself is based upon an elaborate interplay of these symbolic elements, in which multiple signifier substitutions are effected effortlessly, without the individual being aware of it. These substitutions are of the order of metaphor, and the ability of the human mind to comprehend and effect metaphorical substitutions is the basis of functioning within the Symbolic order. When the child submits to the paternal metaphor, it is integrating into its psyche a *way of thinking* that is the template for Symbolic functioning. In addition, the Name-of-the-Father forms the first master signifier, which may be substituted with others as the child develops its Subject and its ego. The Phallus is a represented idea already hidden beneath a representation below the Name-of-the-Father; this 'one-step-removed' version of what is signified gives it great flexibility as a mental structure, because not only is the top layer of the algebraic fraction replaceable with other signifiers, but there is also the possibility of substitutions of the representation below the bar of metaphor, which at the start are repressed into the unconscious. This becomes relevant when studying the role of master signifiers and their link with the object cause of desire and with anxiety.

We can deduce from observation what happens if one or both of the two stages of the submission to the paternal metaphor fail to take place; we can also see what conditions may cause their failure.

First of all, in order for the child to form the hypothesis of the Phallus, the mother must indicate to it that her behaviours are neither whimsical nor persecutory, and that she is only obeying the dictates of some Other. This information will be conveyed in speech, and in normal social settings, other people will also be there to convey this information 'Your mummy had to go to work', etc. Secondly, the paternal signifier must be present in the mother's discourse as a representation of this Other. This does not require the real father to be present – he may be absent either temporarily or permanently, or some other office (work, the mother's current partner, own parents, etc.) may play the role of the Name-of-the-Father – but it must have sufficient power to be a credible representative for the possessor of the Phallus.

There are therefore two possibilities for the failure of the metaphor to happen. If the mother never indicates that her behaviour obeys any exterior requirements or logic, and the child is unable to deduce this, it will be truly locked within a very frightening fantasy based on the dyadic relationship with the mother-Other. This could lead to psychosis. If, however, the child does form the hypothesis of the Phallus, but the mother never speaks the paternal metaphor, then the child may remain in a fantasy that it has or is the Phallus for the mother. In this case as well, the relationship remains dyadic, but now the child may fantasise that it is the lawmaker, the omnipotent and omniscient. This leads to a psychotic structure but not necessarily pure psychosis; this structure is characterised by its difficult relationship with the Law in all its forms, some paranoid elements (as a failure of its will is experienced as persecutory rather than logical in a wider context), and a certain inflexibility with language.

Lacan held that the principal cause of psychosis is the fore-closure of the Name-of-the-Father – that is, the child has never actually 'crossed the bar' into metaphoric functioning. Foreclosure is a Lacanian concept derived from clinical observation of psychotic patients, whose ability to access the metaphor is either limited or completely lacking. To a person in the grip of a psychotic state, the symbolic realm does not exist: everything is frighteningly literal. When the theory of the Name-of-the-Father is applied to child development, one may see how a psychotic structure may emerge as a failure to submit to the paternal metaphor. This may happen in cases where a mother is in a fusional relationship with the child and may never wish to invoke a wider law to which they both must submit, or with a mother who fails to enter into a discourse about her obligations and place in society. It may happen when the mother herself has mental health problems and the child has no alternative carer.

Early childhood psychosis is a condition typically marked by poor language development and some behavioural difficulties; it is a French diagnosis of what in the United Kingdom would be labelled 'autistic'. The crucial difference between early childhood psychosis and autism is that childhood psychosis is something from which the child can recover and catch up to a level where it may function well in society; autism implies a permanent condition. Furthermore, childhood psychosis does not involve a lack of social interactivity or contact, where autism does: the child suffering from early psychosis does make eye contact and may even seek out interaction with others. Autism offers only an organic label; early childhood psychosis seeks out the psychological roots of the syndrome, and Lacan's proposal of the foreclosure of the Name-of-the-Father is particularly helpful in seeing what might have led to the condition and what is required to treat it.

Early childhood psychosis may occur when the child is merely *late* in accessing the symbolic realm: it remains for too long in its enjoyment of the Other as represented by the mother and misses a crucial step in the development of its thinking.

However, even if the child is able to formulate the hypothesis of the Phallus, it may still refuse to submit to the paternal metaphor by clinging to its fantasy that it may have the Phallus, or even be the Phallus for its mother. The symbolic castration is perhaps one of the hardest things for the child to accept, and childhood is liberally dotted about with episodes of regression in which the child passionately refuses to accept that its will does not reign supreme. Moreover, the fantasy of possessing the Phallus is too powerful to banish entirely, especially when it is reinforced from time to time by proofs of how very satisfactory the parents find the child. The incompleteness of the symbolic castration and the persistence of the Phallic fantasy may lead to the development of personality disorders as the child reaches maturity. These include psychopathic or perverse personality disorders that may at times border on delusional states. Symptoms may include megalo-mania, an irrational belief in one's own abilities, some apparently paranoid fantasies, dictatorial and obsessive rule-making, or sometimes simply psychopathic tendencies.

A father with a son who was born HIV-positive tries to prevent him getting the recommended treatment. He loves his son, but he is firmly convinced that he knows better than the experts in whose care the son should be. He is a very religious man, and believes that a combination of prayer and his own home-grown remedies are better, and that tricyclic drugs will endanger his boy. His opposition to the professionals trying to help his son leads to a serious deterioration of the boy's condition and to social services intervention; the man ends up trying to retain custody of his child in court. Even during the legal process, his belief that he is ultimately right and that his decision should be law is so strong that he refuses legal representation, and chooses to fight his own case. He defends his views by saying that he has a medical degree and expertise in pharma-cology, when in reality, he has only a Bachelor's degree in biology and a half-completed diploma as a pharmacist; yet he presents his academic attainments to the court as if he has no understanding of the wider context in which they may be regarded. A psychiatrist diagnoses him as having delusions of grandeur, as well as some paranoid ideation, but he is not psychotic and is able to hold down a job. A Lacanian view would be that his personality has developed around an incomplete castration – that he has a 'psychotic structure', as distinct from being psychotic. In terms of the Name-of-the-Father, although he has been able to gain some degree of 'access to the metaphor' and to understand the existence of a symbolic level of functioning, he has accepted neither that he has not got the Phallus, nor that he is not in a position to make the law.

Even in children who have accepted this symbolic castration, the Phallic Object remains strong in the unconscious: the child may believe the literal truth of Mother's explanation, but 'dinner' and 'work' and even 'Daddy' are never fully satisfactory explanations, and the hypothesis of the Phallus persists, becoming even more mysterious: '*What is it about* Daddy?' may become the basis for the child's identification with the father, as it tries to acquire characteristics that may account for Daddy's ability to draw Mother away. And later on, as the mother's excuses for leaving multiply in accordance with the child's widening grasp of the world, the Phallus will come to exist in these other alibis: *What is it about work that she finds so fascinating? What is it about shopping?* If the Phallus appears most in 'work', then the child who still has some hope of possessing it may throw itself into 'work' in its attempt to discover its mysterious appeal or to absorb its absorbing essence; while the child that has abandoned hope, perhaps because the parents' absorption with work was so intense that it feels that it cannot possibly hope to compete, might set its face against 'work' entirely.

The paternal metaphor as a shield against anxiety

Why does the child accept the paternal metaphor? I have already mentioned the frightening aspect of the mother-as-Other, and how the hypothesis of a third-party Other alleviates that anxiety. But another part of the answer must lie in the prematurity and helplessness of the human infant: lacking the physical possibility of imposing its desire, the child realises that it would be far too painful not to accept the 'solution' of the paternal metaphor. Imagine the child crying for its mother in its cot: she comes in, comforts it and excuses her departure with the paternal metaphor. The child could continue to scream itself to exhaustion, but ultimately, it is easier to accept and 'play the game'. One must not forget how anxiety-making are the mother's absences, or that the opposite of omnipotence is impotence; the reverse side of the child's fantasy of omnipotence, possible while Mother is there to gratify its wishes, is the despair of complete powerlessness and extreme anxiety when faced with the painful truth of infantile incapacity. The Name-of-the-Father/Phallus hypothesis is a shield against anxiety; the failure of the child to accept this could result in anaclytic depression.[4] In accepting the metaphor, the child enters into a '*marché de dupes*' with its mother – a game of complicity in a lie – they both know that the metaphor is a convenience, but a necessary one.

There is yet another advantage for the child in accepting the paternal metaphor: the Name-of-the-Father is something that can be identified with, whose power can be acquired by study and emulation: it is a kind of compensation, a defence against the psychological pain of castration. But there is soon another 'compensation': in the acceptance of castration, the child soon realises that not only has it not got the Phallus, but that *no living person* has; from this point, the Phallus exists in the Imaginary only as a notion – something whose experienced loss is the only 'proof' that it ever existed. It is a lost object, and a property of lost objects is that they may be found. In a later chapter, we shall see how the Name-of-the-Father becomes replaced by master signifiers, and the Phallus by the small a objects, which are the object cause of desire – to be sought after all one's life. Thus it is far better for the child to 'go with' the paternal metaphor than to be constantly defeated by the inexplicability of Mother's behaviours, or its own inability to impose its will upon the exterior world. It has acquired in place of the already-disintegrating fantasy of omnipotence, the solid hope that it can gain by its own powers the lost object of desire, hidden beneath the Name-of-the-Father.

6
Real, Symbolic, Imaginary

Freud postulated a model of the psyche in his Topography: the first consisting of preconscious, unconscious, and conscious, and the second – the one still most commonly used – of ego, id, and super-ego. Lacan's model of the RSI – Real, Symbolic, and Imaginary – is often mentioned in some kind of comparison with this. Those familiar with classical psychoanalytical concepts may try to link or equate Lacanian ideas with those of Freud; they might expect, for instance, that the Symbolic order, which contains laws and signifiers, would correspond to the super-ego, or that the id and the unconscious belong together in the same realm (there has even been a suggestion that Lacan *replaces* the id with the unconscious!). Anyone making the attempt will be confounded in all their assumptions: the unconscious belongs in the Symbolic, and the super-ego and id figure nowhere. The RSI is not analogous with Freud's model: it does not represent the psyche but a system of interacting realms, orders, or registers in which the psyche functions. Where Freud's conception of the human mind always tended towards envisaging it as an interior space, Lacan's Subject is more abstract – it exists 'out there' like a force-field within a universal matrix. The Real, Symbolic, and Imaginary are properties of this matrix and are in every phenomenon associated with the human mind: they provide a framework for the understanding of the normal functioning of human mind, of psychopathology, and also of all human institutions and creations.

Lacan had already been using the concepts of Symbolic and Imaginary for some years before he formulated them into the schema with the Real. He presented the Real, Symbolic, and Imaginary in 1953 – his first presentation immediately after he had resigned from the Société Psychanalytique de Paris, and the idea has remained one of his most important. However, it is also one that is quite hard to pin down – not because it is particularly abstruse (indeed, it is one of the most user-friendly of his concepts) – but because it continued to evolve over the decades, resulting in some inconsistencies. For example, when the Real first appeared in his work, it seemed to be the object of anxiety, but this view changes later; similarly, situating this or that phenomenon 'in' one or another of the RSI realms becomes equivocal because of his formulation of the RSI as a knot made up of the three threads, which suggests that it is, in fact, impossible to entirely disengage a phenomenon from any of the three realms. Moreover, towards the end of his life he added a fourth element – not another order, but something that ties together the three – the *sinthome*.

The Borromean knot of the RSI

Although Lacan's use of the Borromean knot as an analogy came quite late, it is necessary to mention it first to prevent the assumption that the three realms can be thought to function independently of each other – a line of thinking that can only result in frustration, as one follows a thread inevitably to a point where it intersects with another realm. The Borromean knot is so called because it is named after an Italian noble family – Borromeo – who used the formula of interlocking rings in their coat of arms as a symbol of strength in unity. It is a configuration in which the structure would fall apart if any one of the three rings was broken. Figure 1 shows the RSI as interlocking toruses; the use of toruses allows for spaces within each of the rings or realms.

Figure 1 RSI as interlocking toruses

All usual psychological phenomena exist within the spaces between the toruses of this Borromean knot, but psychosis signals its unravelling. Lacan's notions of the Imaginary and the Symbolic are already there in his first paper on the Mirror Stage, and as the Mirror Stage is especially important in the development of the Imaginary realm, and because it denotes the crucial moment at which the baby's Subject is 'split' or alienated from itself and takes on its truly human character, it is a convenient point at which to begin an explanation of the RSI. In early infancy, the functioning of the Imaginary realm is in the forefront, so this is where I shall begin.

The Imaginary

For an understanding of the Imaginary, we must avoid thinking of the word in its commonplace sense of *unreal* or *fictitious* – although there are elements of unreality and fictitiousness within it. We must not be seduced by the 'creative' or 'imaginative' connotations that may attach to the word – although there is a seductive force in the Imaginary, which also contains the foundations of creativity. The Imaginary is named for the mental processes that issue from the encounter between the infant and its image in the mirror; but in order to fully appreciate both the intellectual leap made during the encounter, and the sophistications that flow from it, we must first rewind to a point before the Mirror Stage.

The Imaginary is the realm of the senses in that it houses the conceptions that issue directly from sensorial perception; because of the Mirror Stage, it is also the order of conceptualisations and functioning that proceeds *from the body's image*. The body is the first 'world' of which the baby is aware; before the Mirror Stage, it perceives its body as a collection of fragments – *Is that passing object my hand? What is the meaning of this pressure on my side?* The baby's ability to conceptualise 'my' hand and 'my' side issues from the information it receives via its kinaesthetic, pressure, and pain receptors – none of which are greatly developed in the human infant; also, it may know the sound of its own cry because it associates it with pain. Of all the senses, sight is the one that is best developed in the baby, and it comes to be of the greatest importance in the building of the Subject and its object relations. It is by means of images that the baby recognises its mother, who comes to be represented as the first signifier, and then itself as a *whole* object – in the mirror of her eyes, and then as a reflected image in the real mirror. The images belong in the Imaginary order: they are the clay from which the representations will be fashioned. Thus, at this point, the mother, already recognised in the image of her face, is a kind of proto-representation, pre-dating formal language; the same is true for the baby's own subject self.

Lacan saw the relationship of the Imaginary to the Symbolic as analogous to the relationship between signifieds and signifiers in language; if we remember that the linguistic sign consists of a signifier associated with a signified, we see that the signifier belongs in the Symbolic and the signified belongs to the Imaginary order. Signifiers, I have already said, are the *vorstellungreprasentanzen* – the representations *of ideas*; signifieds are the ideas themselves, and at the age of the Mirror Stage, these are still half-baked and unstable and have not been associated with a signifier drawn from language.

One can see the close connection between sensory perception and the Imaginary in the creation of certain proto-concepts: children with cerebral palsy are often dyspraxic – they have difficulty in performing complex movements and are clumsy and uncoordinated – because without the right degree of sensory 'information', their conceptualisation of three-dimensional space is limited. This ability originates in one's own body and belongs in the realm of the Imaginary; children with severe motor disabilities may only become able to conceptualise space later, through the medium of language.

At the Mirror Stage, through a dialectic of identification with its mirror image, the baby begins to build up its ego or Ideal-I through a projection of ideas upon the object in the mirror. In building conceptions upon something that is both inherently false and powerful – an image – the Imaginary is programmed from the start to be a realm of illusion, and to have a force of fascination and seduction. Certain illusions are necessary for conceptualisation – they form 'proto-concepts' whose function is that of a substratum for the foundation of concepts. Such illusions, according to Lacan, include the abilities to grasp the totality of something, to effect syntheses, and to believe in dualities such as subject/object, exterior/interior, which allow for the functioning of dialectic.

The primal intellectual act of self-recognition is an important moment in the development of the Imaginary realm, because it establishes the individual's narcissism and self-image – the foundations of the ego. In addition, the factitious nature of ego construction and the splitting of the self into subject and object are the templates upon which the functions of synthesis and dialectic are built; these therefore are functions within the Imaginary order, through which we simultaneously figure out and hide reality.

Identification and narcissism define the relationship the baby forms with its mirror image – its '*petit autre*' or small other; identification and narcissism are the means by which it builds up its ego, and also its relationships with all other people. These processes form the basis of like and dislike, love and hate, admiration and disdain, attraction and disgust between Subjects: to simplify a little, it is in the realm of the Imaginary that one sees similarities and differences between oneself and another person, and comes to be attracted or repelled.

As described by Roland Chemama: 'In the relationship between subjects, there is always something false that is introduced – this is the imaginary projection of the one on the screen that the other becomes. The imaginary is the register of the ego with its obliviousness, alienation, love and aggressiveness in the dual relationship with the other.'[1] It is because identification and narcissism belong in the Imaginary that Lacan reproached the major psychoanalytical schools of the day for 'reducing the practice to the Imaginary order'. He felt that the emphasis on counter-transference as an analytical tool made identification with the analyst the objective of analysis (*Ecrits*, 'Directions of the Treatment', 1966): it seems to encourage the interweaving of the Imaginary of the patient with that of the analyst in such a way that finally nothing is elucidated, and the only thing developed is the relationship between the two.

The Symbolic

This is the order that appears at the outset the easiest to imagine and understand, because the word used to describe it remains closest to its common meaning. However, there is a danger in making too many assumptions about it: the Symbolic contains many surprises. For instance, the Phallus, although a ideational 'symbol' of something, is not in the order of the Symbolic but of the Imaginary – to go back to Freud's very useful terminology, it is a *representanz* without a *vorstellung*. The Other – Society, Law, the set of hypotheses within which the Subject is constituted – is not an Imaginary object but a representation of representations, and therefore belongs in the Symbolic; and yet, as the realm of language, which has both a Symbolic and an Imaginary component, it must necessarily sit on the RSI knot at a point which is in contact with the Imaginary. The unconscious, on the other hand, is entirely a thing of the Symbolic, as it is made up of only signifiers, and not signifieds.

Lacan took the term 'Symbolic' from social anthropology, which showed that even the most 'primitive' societies have a symbolic order that regulates kinship, exchanges of goods, and marriages. This order works as a constraint and can be found in pacts of alliance, religious rituals, prohibitions, and taboos; it is also universal to all human society. Lacan extended this concept to embrace all human activity: the Symbolic is manifest in language, laws, and social structures. This is why it is wrong to think of these things as human 'inventions', as if we consciously invented them; rather, for Lacan, they are inherent in our nature, in the Symbolic realm. Hence, the Symbolic order is that of the laws of the *unconscious organisation* of human society.

> If Man brings the symbolic order into being by thought it is because he is already caught up within it. The illusion that he has formed this order within his consciousness stems from the fact that it is through the pathway of a specific gap in his Imaginary relationship with his alter ego that he has been able to enter into this order as a Subject. But he can only enter the Symbolic by means of the straight and narrow path of speech.[2]

Language, the distinguishing characteristic of human beings (*parlêtre*), contains elements belonging in the Symbolic and in the Imaginary. In order for the linguistic sign to be of any use, this relationship must exist, denoted by the Saussurian 'bar'. The originality of the human mind lies in the act of 'crossing the bar' between signifier and signified: this is a natural human ability which doesn't have to be 'learned', and which, in linking the signifier with the signified, makes language possible. Meaning appears at what Lacan called 'stitch-points' – *points de capiton* – between the signifier and signified; in terms of the RSI knot, it could be said to arise where the Symbolic and Imaginary rings touch.

It is signifiers – the *representations* of ideas – and not whole signs, which belong in the Symbolic realm, and it is only by means of representations that things can be conceived of, and by an association of signifiers that meaning appears. Therefore, it is in the realm of the Symbolic that an intellectual apprehension of any phenomenon can be arrived at, and this intellectual apprehension is, at the end of the day, the only truth that matters. This is why Lacan inverted the Saussurian formulation, represented the signifier with a capital S, placed it on top of the bar, and affirmed that the unconscious, and by extension the Subject, are composed of repressed signifiers in a signifying chain, and both therefore belong in the realm of the Symbolic.

'In the Symbolic order, the totality is called a universe. The Symbolic order from the first takes on its universal character. It isn't constituted bit by bit. As soon as the symbol arrives, there is a universe of symbols.'[3] Lacan held that the Symbolic order was always there – like language, it pre-exists the individual, who has to gain access to it. How, then, does this happen?

In Freudian theory, the child develops notions that belong in (what would be) the Symbolic order quite late – at around two years of age; for Lacan, the Symbolic is there, waiting to receive the child, from the moment of its birth. And yet, access to the

Symbolic is fraught with problems: it involves an initiation to which the baby can submit, or refuse. This initiation involves the experience of loss, and plunges the infant first of all into the realm of the Imaginary, which forms at this point a kind of bridge to the Symbolic.

Lacan holds that for the newborn, the 'first signifier' is the maternal signifier, and with it comes the baby's first tenuous foothold in the Symbolic. But how is this first signifier arrived at? How this entry into the Symbolic achieved? From the moment of its birth, the baby experiences a change of environment: something is lost, something is gained, and with this experience, the first sod is dug in the creation of the dialectical foundation, in the realm of the Imaginary. In the first days, the mother is indistinguishable from the 'world' surrounding the child; the mother who breastfeeds and carries the baby close to her body *is* the world for it. But the mother's face – sometimes in the baby's view but sometimes not – introduces anew the dialectic of presence/absence. Via this appearance-disappearance of the mother, the baby becomes aware when she is *not* there, and in doing so, becomes aware of her as an *entity* and not just a part of the environment. But it is the *absence* or the *lack* of the mother that makes her apprehensible as an entity, and this apprehension is, long before the baby is able to say 'mama', the first act of representation of an idea-embodied-in-an-object made by the child – in Freudian terms, the first *vorstellungreprasentanz*, and for Lacan, the formation of the first signifier.

The gaining of access to the Symbolic happens in quantum leaps: the first being the pre-language access to ideational-representatives, as demonstrated in Freud's baby playing with a bobbin, and uttering '*fort-da*' in accompaniment to a game of loss and retrieval. The second leap occurs at the Mirror Stage. It has already been said that this is when the ego is created by the affixation of signifiers to the mirror image – the alter ego; the Subject is the entity, oblivious to itself, which does the affixing; the Subject 'sorts' the signifiers that float about in the discourse of the Other and in doing so invents stories about itself, while simultaneously being completed by the signifiers it represses. The Subject at this stage is largely unconscious, and could be imagined as a force-field reacting with the signifiers of the Other like the charge in a liquid crystal, organising them into chains, repressing some and attaching others to the ego. In its primary function, therefore, the Subject exists in the realm of the Symbolic; 'the Symbolic is the order in which the Subject, as distinct from the ego, comes into being'.[4] The completion of the individual's initiation into the Symbolic comes with the acceptance of the Name-of-the-Father, and of castration.

As we have seen in the formation of the first signifier, Lacan emphasised that 'lack' was essential for access to language, or at least to signifiers; to put it simply, if everything was always present and available to you, you would never need to use language to ask for anything. And because language is the primary human characteristic, the Symbolic order is accessed through the experience of lack, because it designates what has been lost or is missing. From the beginning, this lack is given a meaning through the correlation between what is lacking and the signifier that symbolises it. This aspect of the Symbolic – that 'lack' is essential to its existence – will become important in the understanding of the Real.

The Real

The Real expects nothing, especially not of the Subject, as it expects nothing of speech. But it is there, identical to its own existence, a noise in which one can hear everything, ready to submerge with its splinters what the reality principle has built under the name of external world.[5]

Lacan came up with more 'quotable quotes' about the Real than about any of the other orders, probably because it is by its very nature indescribable. There is always a tendency to lavish words upon what cannot be described, in the hope that some of them might stick – a little like throwing paint in the direction of the Invisible Man in order to make him out. It is not by chance that the Real was the last of his 'realms' to be formulated: the concept was put forward only because in the formulations of the Imaginary and the Symbolic, it became evident that something was always being 'left out'. For Lacan, the Real is what is expelled when a signifier becomes attached to some morsel of reality: it is the bit that the signifier fails to capture. Also, in terms of Hegelian dialectics, the Real must exist in tension with the other two – for something to exist, its inverse must exist as well; and for existence to be, there must also be a state of non-being. Lacan borrowed a term from Heidegger when he said that the Real ex-sists, because the Symbolic and Imaginary exist. More simply (and more usefully in psychoanalysis): for everything that comes into our field of recognition by means of a signifier, something of it must remain imperceptible, unsymbolised: this is the Real.

Lacan described the Real as 'smooth' and 'undifferentiated': 'There are no cracks, no interior or exterior – these distinctions are meaningless in the Real. Only the Symbolic can introduce some cuts in the Real.'[6] The Real is the featureless clay from which reality is fashioned by the Symbolic; it is the chaos from which the world came into being, by means of the Word. 'It is the world of words that creates the world of things, initially mixed up in the here and now of the whole in becoming.'[7]

The Symbolic brings into being all the phenomena of our world: these only exist because they have been symbolised. The Real is best thought of as ineffable and unimaginable – a state perhaps only experienced pre-birth, as even the act of birth introduces a 'cut' in the featurelessness of the baby's universe. Even the newborn has the proto-concept of duality – that there is presence and absence – and by this understanding, it can begin to know that things exist. It is the perceptions of the Imaginary that create ridges and flaws, differences in temperature and texture, interiors and exteriors. Then, the baby learns to attach signifiers to things – which have already made their existence known in the dialectic of presence/absence – and to their properties (hot/cold, hard/soft, nice/horrid); it is these signifiers that bring the world into existence for the child. And yet, the Real persists, in all that cannot be pinned down by a signifier, or by any symbol at all, be it speech, writing, ritual, or art. It is what the Symbolic expels from reality when it forms a representation. Or, as Bruce Fink says, the Real is 'that which resists symbolisation absolutely'; it is 'the domain of whatever subsists outside symbolisation.'[8]

> The Real is something you find always at the same place. However you mess about, it is always in the same place, you bring it with you, stuck to the sole of your shoe without any means of exiling it.[9]

'*Always at the same place*' is one of the properties of the Real, in opposition to the high moveability of the major currency of the Symbolic – signifiers. 'Chair', or 'green', or 'mouse', or 'combustible' may attach themselves to an infinite number of things; but the Real has not that flexibility. Lacan saw the Real in behaviours associated with the death drive and in the repetitive-compulsive element of neuroses. Because it is unsymbolisable, it cannot be transformed and transferred in the way that signifiers may be; but as it too is tied into the Borromean knot, it can be affected by the other two realms. This is important in the understanding of the Real in psychological symptoms such as melancholia or repetition-compulsion: there is something unsymbolised which forms a 'sticking point' in the Subject's functioning, and it is through symbolisation (verbalisation upon the analyst's couch) that this bit of Real may be dealt with.

The character of the Real, being unsymbolisable, is that of absolute terror or absolute enjoyment – both impossible states. Its existence can be postulated by its manifestations. It appears in hallucinations and delusions, when the stitch-points between signifiers and signifieds come apart, where the Borromean ring unravels and the unrepresentable wanders freely in a lake of unattached signifiers. What is remarkable is that when psychosis strikes, it is precisely at the point that some few remaining stitch-points are still holding – where there is still a little contact between the threads of Symbolic and Imaginary – that the symptoms manifest. It is as if, as the knot unravels, in the total terror/total *jouissance* of the Real at large, the Subject clings, by means of its symptom, to the final, weakening but still-recognisable shreds of meaning it can still apprehend.

A mother, in a psychotic episode killed two of her children, because she 'saw the devil in their eyes'. '*Their eyes were black – not normal black – they were the devil's black,*' was one of the statements she offered in explanation. One can imagine the terror of the children in the face of their mother's murderous delusion; one can perhaps *not* imagine (and may not wish to imagine) the terror of the psychotic for whom the Borromean knot has come apart, detaching signifiers from reality, unleashing absolute terror in its pure form to bump at random into hapless signs, which may just contain a sufficient residue of meaning to appear to be some anchor to reality. Hence, the tenuous connection between 'black' and 'devil' is seized upon by the Subject as something it can still understand – some connection it can still make and act upon: but it is precisely because there is still some connection, where all others are falling apart, that it comes to be the unfortunate focus of the psychotic's attention. The unravelling of the knot threatens to annihilate the Subject, whose imperative is to act to preserve itself. This formulation of the symptom being an acting out upon the points at which there is still some attachment between the rings of the unravelling knot may account for the 'meaningfulness' (in the literal sense) of psychotic symptoms observed by psychiatrists as far back as Bleuler. It also led to one of Lacan's last interesting theoretical constructs – the *sinthome*, which we come to shortly.

The Real appears also in psychological trauma. *A tortured Kurdish patient had been having a nightmare over and over again; it remained the same, in every detail, and was a re-experiencing of his real-life experience. In it, the torturer would enter the room and begin to apply the electrodes to his skin. The patient would wake up screaming at the point at which the electrodes touched him.* Lacan would have said that the terrifying quality of the dream was the irruption of the Real that is in helplessness, pain, and mortality. The job of the analyst would be to try to help the patient find signifiers for the unsymbolisable – to allow him to talk in circles around this intrusion of the Real, until at some point he is able to symbolise at least something of it. The Real, of course, is unbanishable; some residue of it will remain, but perhaps an altered residue – in the way an element may be taken up in a chemical reaction, and be combined into a different substance at the end. In this clinical instance, the patient carried on having the dream and talking about it, until one day, the dream occurred again – but with an alteration: the scene remained the same, except that the torturer, when he entered, had the head of a dog. The patient was baffled by this until the analyst said, in agreement with his almost-conscious knowledge: '*These people are indeed real animals.*' The character with the dog-head was a creation of the Imaginary realm, but the interpretation was in the Symbolic, because it translated the image into the signifier 'animals' which revealed the hidden message. Whatever the nature of the Real in the dream before this transformation and interpretation, it was not the same afterwards, because the dream ceased to have its full terrifying effect. Some transformation of the Real can be said to have taken place – some 'chemical synthesis' in which it was combined with elements of the Symbolic and Imaginary.

To begin with, Lacan thought that the Real was the object of anxiety: 'the essential object which isn't an object any longer, but this something faced with which all words cease and all categories fail, the object of anxiety par excellence'.[10] Later on, he came to associate anxiety with the small a object (*l'objet petit a*), which is explained in chapter 8.

Although Lacan does not say this, it seems consistent with his ideas of the Real to suggest that the drives (German *trieb* and *instinkts* and French *pulsions*) belong in this realm. Freud had posited the existence of an erotic or libidinal drive, which tends towards creation and pleasure; to account for the fact that so much of human behaviour appears to counter this, he postulated the death drive, and also the drive for self-preservation. In Lacan's 1959 seminar on Pleasure and Reality, there is an indication that he places the drives in the Real in the words in which he describes the death drive: 'Beyond the pleasure principle we encounter that opaque surface which to some has seemed so obscure that it is the antimony of thought – not just biological but scientific in general – the surface that is known as the death instinct'.[11] The death drive could manifest as pleasure-seeking to begin with, but distinguishes itself in the way that a person who seeks the pleasure of a glass of a good wine is distinct from the person who seeks oblivion in a bottle of hard liquor. As an interesting aside, Lacan linked aggression with the drive for self-preservation and not with the death drive: apart from cases of perversion, one is usually aggressive in the preservation of the ego rather than because one simply enjoys an act of destruction.

Drives are the 'featureless clay' of instinct that Lacan has banished from the unconscious. They do not have as a goal the satisfaction of some biological need. They exist quite independently of need; like a kind of engine, their satisfaction lies merely in the functions they propel, and the enjoyment produced by the function connected with a drive is what Lacan calls *jouissance*.

Drives are unsymbolisable and the passions to which they give rise through the mediation of the Imaginary remain difficult to capture with signifiers. 'Anxiety', 'anger', and 'fear' are relatively stable in their meanings, and even they have a slippery quality about them. Other emotional signifiers are even more weakly joined to any signified: who can truly say what it is to 'love' someone, or to be 'happy', or 'excited', or 'depressed'? The weakness of the stitch-points between signifiers and signified in the area of emotions may be because of the unrepresentable nature of the drives from which they arise.

Various examples of the RSI at work

We have already spoken a little of the Borromean knot of the RSI. In talking about each individual torus within it, one may forget that psychological phenomena are created by the knot itself, at points where the realms come into contact. Every human creation contains all three rings, even if one predominates over another; take art as an example.

Because the Imaginary is the realm of the senses, much of representative art contains a great amount of Imaginary: it is in the sensuous quality of paintings of draped robes, the glitter of frost, warm brickwork, etc. One can easily discern to what extent the Imaginary is being granted importance in the look of an artwork. Before the Renaissance, the Imaginary in art was held somewhat in abeyance: ideas and their symbols – mostly with a strongly religious flavour – took such great precedence over the realm of the senses that not even perspective was deemed important, let alone perceptions even more intimately linked with the body. In conceptual art, once again, the Symbolic comes to the fore: it is *what can be said* of an item that matters – the ideas it evokes, rather than the sensuous response. Another simple example can be seen in the contrast between Western and Chinese gardening: the Western gardener who cultivates the softest, lushest lawn is pandering to the fantasies of the Imaginary; the Chinese one who constructs a pile of rockwork to represent the mountain-lair of gods and propitious spirits is functioning almost entirely in the realm of the Symbolic.

The RSI can be found in the commonest examples of human activity. A girl buying 'pampering products' – moisturisers, body creams, bath salts, aromatherapy oils – is a good example of someone in search of a small a object, which sits in the Borromean knot of the Symbolic, the Imaginary, and the Real. She imagines, somehow, that these products contain the object cause of desire of some perfect imaginary state. The Imaginary creates the sensuous fantasy involved with skin, softness, warmth; the Symbolic extracts that into words, and piles on many other signifiers that have nothing to do with the product in question – to the point that it often seems that the purchaser is buying signifiers. However, the Real is present too, '*stuck to the sole of your shoe*' as Lacan would have it – for what motivates the purchase must be the anxiety attached to the loss of the perfect state and also the (libidinal) drive – both of which belong in the Real.

The *sinthome*

We have already mentioned that in the unravelling of the Borromean knot that occurs in a psychotic episode, the delusion usually appears still to have some meaning to the Subject, and that it manifests precisely at the stitch-points at which the RSI orders are still connected. This observation may have contributed to Lacan's formulation of the construct he named the *sinthome*.

The word *sinthome* is an old French spelling for symptom, and this idea is one that Lacan came to very late in life: he taught it in his seminar of 1975–76. *Sinthome* designates the structural aspect of symptoms, which are its observable manifestations. It may be useful here to describe the context in which symptoms are usually understood in psychoanalysis.

Freud first noted that many symptoms displayed by patients had a psychological rather than a biological origin; Bleuler hypothesised that symptoms, even psychotic delusions, have meaning for the patient. Lacan's reflections on the matter were to begin with an elaboration of the classical hypothesis that the treatment of symptoms lay in their interpretation, and that the elucidation of their meaning would result in a 'curing' of the patient. In his theoretical trajectory, he reflected upon the mechanism and process by which this curing comes about, thereby arriving at his theories of the role of language in the structure of the Subject. In 1957, he had come to the view that a Subject's symptom came into being in the process of the formation of the unconscious, and that this process involved acts of language, or discourse: the symptom is 'inscribed in a writing process'.[12] This was directly in line with his reflections upon the role of language in the formation of the Subject and it clearly situates the symptom within the structure of the Subject; by implication, as a product of language, the symptom is also excisable only by discourse.

But soon, Lacan became preoccupied by a different, albeit related matter: what exactly does 'curing' mean? Is it simply the disappearance of a symptom, or does one aim to change the underlying personality structure that produced it and *in which it is inscribed*? Is this at all achievable, and if it is, is it desirable? If it is neither achievable nor desirable, then where should curing stop – at what boundary line? And finally, is it always a good thing even to begin the process, when you don't know where to end it or whether you will be leaving behind a damaged and less effective Subject?

We may all look around us and notice acquaintances who have obvious (although never to themselves) neurotic symptoms – a woman locked into an unhappy marriage for no material reason, a man in love with a manipulative and selfish woman, a gardener so obsessed with his allotment that he cannot even allow himself to go on holiday for a week – but we know intuitively not to meddle with their symptoms, *especially* not to point out any 'home truths', for fear of the damage this 'wild interpretation' (as Lacan would have called it) might wreak in their lives.

By the early 1960s, Lacan felt that forcing people to confront the truth about themselves, the meaning of their symptoms and the hitherto repressed elements in their unconscious, had consequences too serious to be undertaken with anything less than the greatest caution.

> The Freudian unconscious is situated at that point where, between cause and that which it affects, there is always something wrong … what the unconscious does is to show us the gap through which neurosis recreates a harmony with a real – a real that may well not be determined. Once this gap has been filled, is the neurosis cured? After all, the question remains open. But the neurosis becomes something else – sometimes a mere illness, a scar. As Freud said – this scar, not of the neurosis, but of the unconscious.[13]

Those last two sentences suggest that sometimes neurosis is preferable to the 'illness', the scarring its removal would leave.

Lacan's decades of clinical observation and preoccupation with the ethics of psychoanalysis led him to a surprising view of the symptom that is best explained in terms of the RSI orders, although I must first add a final word relating to the symptom as something inscribed in the Subject. If the symptom is indeed so intimately connected with the structure of the Subject's personality or psyche, then its removal would necessarily leave a scar – the foundation of the house which has been demolished. It is this – the structural foundation of the symptom – that Lacan calls the *sinthome*, in one of his most arcane seminars near the end of his life.

In terms of the RSI, Lacan saw the symptom as the effect of elements within the Symbolic realm (for the most part, signifiers) upon the Real of the body, the drives, etc. As a quick and easy example, one could think of a symptom such as soiling in children who are past a nappy-wearing age: it is not difficult to see the connection between the signifiers produced by the angry parent or authority figure in a sentence such as, '*Can you stop being such a baby?*' and the child's use of the part drive (control) and its attendant function (anal) to insist upon his status as a child. This is in no way intended as a generalisation upon the meaning of this particular symptom, which will be different in every case, only as an illustration of the way in which signifiers from the Symbolic may interact with the drives of the Real.

In his seminar in 1975–76, Lacan suggested a modification of his Borromean knot, introducing into it a fourth circle – the *sinthome*, whose role is to hold the knot in place, so preventing any unravelling of the Imaginary, Symbolic, and Real. Thus, the *sinthome* in fact provides stability to the system. This seminar has been of great interest to students of English, because in it, Lacan goes into some detail about the work of James Joyce, whom he views as having a potentially psychotic personality structure in which the Borromean knot is prevented from unravelling by his writing. Only Joyce's peculiar relationship with his art allowed him to keep meaning and being together, and in this respect, his writing was a prosthesis – a *sinthome*.

The *sinthome* is inscribed in the Subject as a signifier chain, and it is through the action of this specific configuration that it acts upon the Real to produce the symptoms. Lacan also held that the *sinthome* was that which allowed the Subject to experience enjoyment – the kind of enjoyment linked with drives (which will be explained in chapter 7). This enjoyment is a component of desire – the desire that Lacan held to be a structural force in the Subject – and cannot be removed. These are complex concepts that can only be understood after *jouissance* (enjoyment) and desire have been explained, and the *sinthome* will be revisited towards the end of the book when this has been done.

Lacan clarified his position about patients and symptoms, saying that while it is reasonable that individuals expect their symptoms to disappear following an analytical treatment, it might not be prudent to try to suppress the use of the fourth circle of the Borromean knot. If the *symptom* must 'fall' during the treatment, the *sinthome* should stay but become modified in such a way that enjoyment and desire remain possible – a little like strengthening and deepening the foundations of the demolished house so that a better one can be built upon them. I shall finish with an example of a patient who, at the end of her treatment, seemed quite aware of the loss she would suffer as a result of being cured.

The young woman, who had been severely anorexic, talked about a dream during one of her last sessions. In it, she had on a necklace on which there was a great, pointed spike or barb. The curious thing was that this necklace was under her skin, within her body, and she wanted to remove it – to get it out of her. She somehow managed to tug it out, but as the spike came out of her body, it left a gaping hole, and she was bleeding. The analyst said in agreement with her unconscious knowledge: '*Yes, you will be left with a hole. And you will be bleeding.*' The patient understood immediately and perfectly the meaning of both: that the giving up of her symptom would indeed leave a hole in the structure of her Subject, and she would face the new reality of menstrual bleeding. If this illustration leaves one with many questions, that is as Lacan would have wished.

Unspeakable need, unquenchable desire
Need, speech, and desire

You can't always get what you want,
But if you try sometimes
You just might find
You get what you need.

(Mick Jagger, 1968)

Desire has a special place in Lacan's work; at times, he seems to focus upon it to the exclusion of other affects. But to Lacan, desire was more a condition than an affect; he did not talk very much about 'affects', perhaps because unless one knows precisely what is talking about, one may end up in a dialogue of the deaf. His method was to examine in close detail and depth a phenomenon in its singularity: rather than filing it into a category whose rigours are untested, he would involve himself in intense reflection upon its nature and origins, how it comes into being (he liked the expression '*inscribes itself*') in the Subject, what part it plays in the structure of the Subject, and how it plays this part (i.e. the mechanisms by which it makes its mark).

I would suggest three reasons he chose to focus such attention upon desire: firstly, desire seemed to figure large in his own personality; he must have been aware of the strength of his own desires – for nice things, fast cars, beautiful women, recognition, knowledge, and to find the answers to his own myriad questions. Secondly, desire is the mainspring of all creativity:

without desire, there would be no human advancement. Thirdly and perhaps most importantly, he saw desire as a *condition that plays a structuring role in the Subject*; it is a component of other affects – without desire, you cannot have jealousy, anger, disappointment, narcissistic wounding, or enjoyment. Symptoms including repetition compulsion, hysterical conversions, obsessions, and phobias, all arise from desire; desire is always at the root of whatever problem the analysand is experiencing, and the patient's desires are both the object of the analysis, and its motor force.

Some readers may feel that Lacan may be over-stating the importance of desire: *but surely*, they may say, *there are other affects that are as important, such as anxiety?* Indeed anxiety occupies as central a role as desire, but for Lacan, this exists in a kind of tension with desire: where there is anxiety there is desire.

Desire is the desire of the Other

> Desire is what manifests itself in the interval demand excavates just shy of itself, insofar as the subject, articulating in the signifying chain, brings to the light his lack of being with his call to receive the complement of this lack from the Other – assuming that the Other, the locus of speech, is also the locus of this lack.[1]

Lacan is saying here that when a Subject is moved to make a demand, it signals a neediness – a lack of something – and expects to receive from the Other the complement – the precise thing – that will fill this lack and complete it; however, what is demanded is never what is actually needed, and it is in this space between need and demand that desire appears. Furthermore, Lacan continues, in making the demand, the Subject assumes that the Other has whatever it needs, while in fact the Other is as lacking as the Subject.

Lacan then continues:

- if desire is an effect in the subject of the condition ... that his need pass through the defiles of signifiers;
- and if ... we must establish the notion of the Other as being the locus of speech's deployment ...

then it must be posited that man's desire is the Other's desire.[2]

In other words, because it is only in speech that the demand can be made, it follows that the Other will define the parameters of the Subject's demand: the articulation of need must pass through the narrow gateway of language and what cannot squeeze through and is left behind constitutes desire. The idea of desire as the desire of the Other is one of the most difficult to explain in the Lacanian canon, but here are a few key precepts to bear in mind, which I will expand upon later, one at a time.

- Desire is the by-product of language, in the Other, and is the result of the impossibility that demand can fully articulate the need.
- Desire is in itself desirable; there is a close link between desire and *jouissance* (enjoyment), which seems to lend something of its self-sustaining nature to desire.
- The Other is first of all language and the set of rules that govern the Subject, but it is *also represented by individuals*. At the start of one's life, there is only one Other, embodied by the mother (and at castration, father); later, the Subject will encounter other Others, embodied in other others (usually the Subject's peer group). As the Subject is moulded by the discourse of the Other, it will fabricate, out of all these Others, its own version of the Other and its own authentic desire, and it is this above all that is the prize in its quest for self-determination.
- The objects around which desire is organised are imaginary objects: the *objet petit a* (small a object, also called 'the object

cause of desire'); the Phallus, and the Thing. The *objet petit a* is a symbolised version of the Phallus, and strictly speaking, the Thing is not an object cause of desire but the object of loss; nonetheless, it is an object towards which affects gravitate, and which desire often circles.

- The *objet petit a* sits on the Borromean knot at the point where the realms of Symbolic, Imaginary, and Real come into contact. It is a product of the drives of the Real, the objects of the Imaginary and the structuring force of the signifiers in the Symbolic.

How desire arises from the impossibility of demand

'Desire appears at the margin where demand is torn from need.'[3] Demand is spoken and yet what you ask for is never what you truly want, as what you want is something that remains hidden from your consciousness; so it is with the acquisition of language that desire arises.

At first, the baby cries out of discomfort, but doesn't know what it needs; as it acquires language, it tries to 'solve' its discomfiture by using the words in its lexicon. To begin with, the baby knows only a few words that seem understood by others, and in its attempt to have its need met, it may say '*bottle*' or '*mama*' or '*bear*', while what it really needs may be something quite different or even something that doesn't exist. But these signifiers have predetermined signifieds imposed by language, and so the baby has to accept these as the solution to its need, however unsatisfactory. Anyone can observe the frustration of the toddler as it finds that whatever it asks for just isn't doing the trick: *milk, banana, bear, train*, and even *mama* get rejected with increasing impatience until finally, the child gives up and settles for one of these substitutes, whimpering with unsatisfied desire.

From the very outset of acquiring language, the verbalisation of need elicits stuff (service, objects) predetermined by the relationship between signified and signifier, and these things are never quite what is wanted. It is in the space between demand and need that desire appears. This 'desire gap' does not go away as the child's language becomes more sophisticated, because the child's needs become increasingly complex too, and its ability to express them confounded by increasing internal conflicts. Furthermore, there are *needs for which no demand can be issued* and also *non-needs for which no demand is appropriate*. The relationship between need and desire can be expressed in the simple statement: *one needs what is essential, but one desires what is not* (one *needs* water to survive, but one *desires* a Gucci handbag). This begs three questions: why does one desire? Whence does desire arise? And by what mechanism and process? For Lacan, the answers to these lay in language, the Other.

Desire grows around objects that fulfil a psychological need, rather than a physical one: it grows most strongly around the objects around which the Subject is constructed. It is strengthened by the difficulty experienced in formulating a demand that will match the psychological need, which, unlike physical thirst or hunger, is not easy to justify. This is particularly true of the demands that issue from the need for love, because by its very nature love is inexpressible in language, and is the greatest of the psychological needs. Lacan held that every demand is essentially a demand for love.

At first, the baby appears only to need milk, attention to its hygiene, and rest. Psychoanalysis has made much of the breast, because it is a perfect object for the newborn baby: it is food, drink, warmth, comfort, and love. The newborn, drunk on milk, hardly knows it's been born. Psychoanalysts point to that state of contentment as something that can never be found again, they point to the breast as a lost perfect object, although not in the same way that the Phallus is a lost perfect object. But that perfect state cannot persist, because the child is growing, and as it does so, its needs become more complex. After a while, it needs to use its developing muscles, and it needs stimulation. Those needs can be met quite easily: a safe room with space to crawl about, furniture to hold onto so that it may pull itself onto its feet, a television and a couple of toys should suffice ... but they don't.

Studies in the early part of the twentieth century of institutionalised babies showed that even when adequately cared for, they failed to thrive: they became listless and depressed and some began to fall behind severely in their cognitive development. Lacan – and perhaps everyone else – would say that from day one, the child also needs love, but this begs the question *why*; love is, anyway, a lot of different things, so what aspect of love is it here, that is so essential to the formation of the child's mental health? The answer may lie in Lacan's Mirror Stage, in which the mother's loving gaze is the child's first mirror and crucial to the formation of the infant's sense of identity.

If you cast your mind back to chapter 2, you may remember how the failure of this first mirror can lead to a deep fault in the foundation of the baby's sense of identity, which is the ability to conceive of itself as an object, and a beloved object. Without the means of forming the proto-concept of 'self' at the right moment in infancy, there may be severe delays in cognitive development or even a complete failure to develop the concept of 'subject' and by extension 'object' and all the conceptualisations that follow, resulting in severe autism. All this would imply that 'love' is a primary need – perhaps *the* primary need – with respect to the construction of the human Subject.

But it is in the dimension of love that demand can never 'match' the need, and therefore the dimension in which desire flourishes. One can only demand love obliquely, because in its very nature, it eludes language. It is not that the child does not *try* to ask for it, indeed, once a child is able to speak, most of its demands *are* expressions of its need for love. If you think about it, outside circumstances of extreme economic hardship (in the developing world or in war), it is rare for a child to have to demand something fundamental to its physical survival. Most of the time, what it asks for is 'extra': every day and at every opportunity, '*plain* pasta not filled' or 'chocolate cake' or 'not the yoghurt with bits in but *that* one'. It is in the inessential 'extra' that is coded the demand for love: in Lacan's words, 'the demand cancels the particularity of whatever is given by changing it into a proof of love'.[4]

But why cannot love be demanded directly? Lacan would say that it is because love consists in 'giving what one doesn't have' (*Ecrits*) – in other words, it can only be seen in the effort put in by the giver of love. Thus, the child 'deduces' the mother's love by the effort and will she puts into satisfying the inessential part of the demand; her love is read in her proofs that *her greatest desire* is to be with and satisfying to the child. In this relationship, therefore, the child sees the mother's love as depending upon the existence of a need (Lacan calls it a lack-in-being) and a desire *in her* – a desire the child thinks it fulfils.

Sexual desire grows from a lack of need

The second principal focus of desire is sex. Imagine, if you will, a bad film in which some lost traveller limps out of a desert towards a solitary house, crawls up the front steps and croaks out a plea for water; it is quite likely that the householder will give him water and perhaps food as well. The same scenario could not work if the traveller's demand was, 'Sex! Or I shall die!' – except, perhaps in some absurdist context.

The fact is, the sexual drive (the 'part drive' whose object is the genitalia) is one with no real *need* attached to it: one can go through one's entire life without having sex and remain perfectly healthy. There are perhaps those who would say, 'but sex is necessary for the continuation of the species' – yes of course, but this is need at a population level and does not concern the individual, who is also perfectly capable of having sex without procreating. As a drive with an object but no need, the sex drive therefore provides fertile ground for the seeds of desire, as there can be no demand that arises from it that is justifiable with a physical need.

The components of desire – drives and enjoyment

It is necessary at this point to talk a little about drives and objects, but readers with a background in classical psychoanalysis must be warned that to follow the lines of thought taken by mainstream psychoanalysis and its related branches towards 'object relations theory' will be futile in understanding the Lacanian model; indeed to do so would be to try to fit a square peg into a round hole. Lacan did not make much use of the notion of 'part drives' or 'part objects', and only mentioned them in passing, because they were the 'psychoanalytical currency' of the day. This digression is therefore aimed at just defining a few terms as they will aid in explaining Lacan, and not in their full development within other branches of psychoanalysis.

I have already mentioned in chapter 4 that the drives or instincts (erotic, self-preservative, and the death drive) belong in the realm of the Real. There are, besides these (or as a sub-set of these) what Freud called partial drives, which manifest themselves in the functioning of a particular physical aspect of the organism (mouth, anus, genitalia), by means of the vehicle of an object. Thus, the object of the oral drive is the breast, of the anal drive the faeces, and the phallic drive, the genitalia.

(Freud's use of the word 'phallic' here is totally different from Lacan's employment of it as a purely imaginary creation linked with power; Freud literally meant 'penis', linked with sexual gratification).

Drives are what causes the organism to exercise a function in which a part of the organism acts upon an object: the oral drive is what causes the baby to suckle the breast, the drive that has been labelled 'anal' is actually the controlling instinct whose object (the stool) is something that may be 'lost' from the Subject, and which control will retain. Drives are independent of need. The functioning of the oral drive is observable even *in utero*: in the last stages of pregnancy, the unborn baby can be seen sucking its thumb, showing that the functioning of the expressive apparatus of the drive has begun even before the need that comes to be associated with it has entered the organism's life. And as Lacan points out, even in adult life, it is the drive that is satisfied in the eating of tasty food, *not* the biological need, which can be satisfied independent of taste or even by bypassing the mouth altogether: 'Even when you stuff your mouth – the mouth that opens in the register of the drive – it is not the food that satisfies it, it is, as one says, the pleasure of the mouth.'[5]

Once the baby is born, needs come into its life, and there arises the triangular relationship between drive, object, and need – and in the wake of need, language. As I noted in chapter 3, language is acquired by the child in order to fulfil need – if there was never a need to ask for something, it would not need to speak; another way of looking at it is that need *justifies* the demand, which is, in fact, usually aimed at the satisfaction of something (I remain deliberately vague at this point) for which there is no proper justification. We only have to look at the commonplace situation of the person at a restaurant hesitating over the menu to witness the linkage of drive, the anticipated enjoyment of it, the justification of this unjustifiable enjoyment with need, and the desire that grows in the space in between.

It is observable that the functioning of the part of the body linked with the drives (oral, anal, genital) is enjoyable in itself, even in the absence of need – as seen with the thumb-sucking *in utero*, the over-eating of non-essential food, or more importantly, in sexual acts. Sex is simply not justifiable with need, and where there is no need, what exactly does one demand? And here, we have reached a similar but different problematic as exists with love – the difficulty of formulating demand. The difference between love and sex in their relationship with demand is that love cannot be demanded because it can only be deduced by the efforts to give what is not materially needed, and yet it answers a real psychological need. Sex, by contrast, *can* be demanded but meets no justifiable need either physical or psychological, and why should you ask for something you don't need, except as a proof of love?

The Subject's enjoyment of the functioning of the physical apparatus linked with the drive does not reduce tension, but sustains it, and it is in this enjoyment, disassociated from need, that we must look for a further factor in the genesis of desire. Lacan introduced into psychoanalysis the term *jouissance*, which is usually translated as 'enjoyment' or 'usage' in English; it attracts controversy in the French-speaking world because its most commonplace meaning has the sexual connotation of 'orgasm' – which is absent in the English translations. However, in French, *jouissance* is also a legal term denoting the right of someone to enjoy the legitimate use of a property – it is exactly the same as the English legal term in phrases such as 'the right of the householder to the quiet enjoyment of his property'. In Lacanian thought, *jouissance* has the advantage of denoting *not* the satisfaction that arises from the attainment of a goal, but a form of enjoyment derived from the usage of something in its legitimate (intended) way – the pleasure that comes with the functioning of the physical or psychological apparatus associated with a drive. This distinguishes this type of enjoyment from the pleasure obtained from the satisfaction of a need, which, unlike *jouissance,* does reduce tension.

Jouissance is the enjoyment of a sensation for its own sake, and is linked with the death drive, which goes beyond the pleasure principle. An illustration of the link between *jouissance* and the death drive would be the case of a drug addict or alcoholic, who seeks *jouissance* by pushing the sensation given by the drug a step further to the point of death; another example might be the case of extreme anorexics.

Because of the early link of *jouissance* with the functioning of parts of ourselves in an instinctive way, one might be tempted to conclude that *jouissance* belongs entirely to the realm of the senses – the Imaginary – but for the purposes of explaining desire, Lacan situates it in the Symbolic. Why?

One may answer this by reference to the anal function, which provides a clear illustration of the point. The function itself, as well as the drive to control, are present from birth, but initially the Subject is not conscious of its anal functioning (unlike its oral functioning, of which the baby becomes aware very early indeed). It is only at the point at which the Subject becomes aware firstly that its body 'loses' something (the stool), and then that it is within its ability to retain this something by means of a body part that may be consciously controlled, that the act associated with the anal function becomes a source of *jouissance*. The anal function comes *to represent* the notion of the 'loss' and retention of something from oneself. It is through this function that the child becomes conscious of its power of control, and (especially if the child's parents make a fuss about 'potty training') of the power of its ability to control other people. In other words, it is only when the anal function has become laden with significance (it has entered the realm of the Symbolic) that the child experiences enjoyment (*jouissance*) in it.

Jouissance, as distinct from pleasure, is the experience that elicits desire; pleasure, in reducing tension, responds to a need, where *jouissance* is an unjustifiable condition. It may in part be from *jouissance* that desire derives its characteristic of wishing to sustain itself.

Jouissance is not suffering, but suffering often plays a part in it. Freud's classic example of the infant playing with an object on a string which it 'loses' and pulls back, uttering the famous '*fort-da*' in accompaniment of the repeated losses and retrievals,[6] is an example of the functioning of *jouissance*. The suffering of loss is as important a part of the game as the satisfaction of retrieval; indeed, the suffering is necessary for *jouissance* to be possible, as the simple presence of the object in the bed would not produce satisfaction.

The infant's primitive verbalisation in this game is also important: the vocalisation of '*fort-da*' represents the child's attachment of symbolic elements to the otherwise meaningless comings and goings of the bobbin. The signified concepts are already present in the child's mind, and it is the exercise of these concepts, via the vocalisation, that produces pleasure in the game. In this case, *jouissance* is derived from the functioning of the psychological apparatus – the mind of the child that is beginning to apprehend and play with dualistic concepts, and which can combat the anxiety produced by loss with its knowledge that it can make the object return. This is quite a complex level of conceptualisation, and is neatly encapsulated in the two syllables uttered by the infant. This process of symbolisation is the means by which drives may be enjoyed in a sublimated form: 'Sublimation is nonetheless satisfaction of the drives, without repression.'[7]

For Lacan, there is also another relationship between *jouissance* and the Other: he thought that pleasure is arrived at by the limitation of *jouissance* by the Other. 'There is a primitive relationship of knowledge to jouissance and this is ... what emerges at the moment where the signifier appears.'[8] This underlines the unconscious element of *jouissance*, which only becomes a recognised pleasure when it is symbolised. For example, a mother might observe that her daughter has been wriggling for a while, doing that 'pre-toilet dance' because she is enjoying 'holding it in', and say: '*For goodness sake, Jane, just go to the toilet!*' – which then allows the child to take the pleasure that comes with the release of tension. Usually, the child is truly unconscious of her need and her state of tension until language, the Other, comes in to express it.

'Otherly' enjoyment and Phallic enjoyment

Before the infant accesses the paternal metaphor, it supposes that the mother is there entirely for its satisfaction, and it enjoys this mother-object, who is the whole and highly satisfactory world to it; at the same time, it has identified the mother as the representative of Other – the Omnipotent and Omniscient – and itself with her. Its identification with her at this stage is so intense that it experiences her as the powerful part of itself. Lacan described the infant's psychological position at this point as being in '*la jouissance de l'Autre*' (the enjoyment of the Other) or '*l'Autre jouissance*' (Otherly enjoyment). This text prefers the latter term, as giving it the definite article seems to suggest that it belongs in the realm of the Symbolic, when it is so clearly in that of the Imaginary: the Other referred to is a proto-Symbolic Other, as the child has not clearly situated it outside its dyadic relationship. Furthermore, the child's enjoyment of this Other is based upon its fantasy of omnipotence as conferred by its identification with the mother – an untenable albeit attractive state.

L'Autre jouissance is what can be observed in babies and small children; echoes of it remain in all of us. The infant is entirely sensualist and self-centred in its 'Otherly' enjoyment; it believes the objective world to be designed for its satisfaction, and that its will reigns supreme. However, at some point, this fantasy will be severely curtailed by the submission to the paternal metaphor and the infant's entry into the Symbolic realm, in which it learns to take a different form of enjoyment – *la jouissance phallique*.

When a child begins to function well in the Symbolic realm – the realm of language, laws and all the social constructs that arise from these – it is the access to Phallic enjoyment that allows it to learn to read; to take pleasure in structured games in which there are rules (as opposed to purely physical play); to be able to include more and more elements of the real world in its imaginary games; to appreciate humour in which the joke consists in overturning rules of language or society; and to understand puns and clever rhymes where an appreciation of the underlying rule is necessary for the thing to work. The child at this stage will become interested in learning, and will start to develop its grown-up theories of the universe. All these things are manifestations of its Phallic enjoyment. But what is the impetus for the child to enter into Phallic enjoyment? Why should its symbolic castration make it go down this route? The answers to these questions are at the heart of the building of the Subject and its ego, and in them one may find the status of desire in the formation of the Subject.

Anxiety, desire, and the Phallus

The absences or 'disobedience' to the child of the mother (who is busy pursuing her own desire) are the cause of great anxiety and rage in the child: still relatively helpless, its fantasies of omnipotence (when mother is there and attentive) are damaged by the reality of its impotence (when she is not, or refuses it what it wants). The supposition that the mother is seeking the Phallus in her absence, or obeying its dictates when she goes against the will of the child, makes it the ultimate object of desire for the child, by this sequence of unarticulated thoughts:

1 *It must be a wonderful thing if she spends so much time on it – it must be desirable in itself; also, it must be a powerful thing if she must obey it, even more powerful than she is* – the child's desire forms around the Phallus.

2 *Maybe if I can get it, then she will want to be with me and I will not have to face her absences and I will get whatever I want* – the Phallus as an attainable object and a defence against anxiety.

After it has formulated in the Imaginary the hypothesis of the Phallus, the child may, for a period, cling to the hope that *it* has the Phallus (which is proven by the mother's presence), but if castration is successful and complete, then it relocates the Phallus in association with (hidden beneath) the Name-of-the-Father, in an act of symbolisation. Then, in accepting its barred (castrated) state ($), the child begins to seek the lost Phallus, which is now attachable to all manner of signifiers, in the exterior world (in its *object relations*, in the jargon of psychoanalysis).

As we have seen, the acceptance of the paternal metaphor is a way out of the impasse of its real impotence in the face of Mother's absence or disobedience, and for two additional reasons: because the Phallus is relocated 'elsewhere' as a lost object, it or something of it is retrievable again; and because one may aspire, in identifying with the Name-of-the-Father, to gaining it. Because the Name-of-the-Father is a signifier, it is infinitely replaceable with others; the Phallus is an idea of the ultimate object of desire, attached to a representation that is in the unconscious but is also replaceable. In other words, if you retrace the path towards the metaphor:

Name-of-the-Father (O)
————————————————
Phallus

you arrive back at the original formulation:

$$\frac{S1}{\text{signifier of object of mother's desire (S')}} \over \text{signified object of mother's desire}$$

in which, as you can see, there are two replaceable signifiers, S1 and S' (which was shoved into the unconscious); this allows the object of desire to take on myriad representations, both conscious and unconscious.

What the child supposes the Phallus to be for its mother will depend upon her real desires: a mother who is highly sociable and constantly in company may have a child who thinks that the object of her desire is contained in the concept of 'sociability' or 'popularity'; a mother who is a piano teacher and whose object of desire seems to be enshrined in the ability to play the piano may have a child who, in his quest for the Phallus, becomes a concert pianist. The desire to possess the Phallus is the motor behind much of human activity, which keeps at bay the anxiety that arises out of the acceptance of one's lack of it.

Castration brings with it a new psychological need – that of possessing the Phallus, the metaphorical object of desire which will ensure the Subject's own desirability; the Phallus now serves as the new object of the libidinal drive, whose organs of expression are not only the genitalia but also the intellect. There is just as much, if not greater *jouissance* in the functioning of the mind than in the functioning of any other bodily part. The ability to cross the bar of metaphor, to operate in the symbolic realm – to conceptualise, to analyse, and to rationalise – are all libidinal functions, which entail enjoyment of the mere functioning of the intellect. One can observe in children who have just successfully integrated the laws of language the enjoyment they derive from reading and other Symbolic activities. Nonsense rhymes, limericks, and puns are screamingly funny for children (and adults) who fully understand the rules of language and society that are being broken. This is *jouissance*, rather than pleasure, for no tension is reduced, and often they try to sustain it for as long as they can, piling joke upon joke, until the rules collapse, and the enjoyment dissipates. Phallic enjoyment is every bit as powerful a component of desire as that related to a bodily function; as Lacan rather pithily said: 'I am not fucking, I am talking to you. Well! I can have exactly the same satisfaction as if I were fucking. That's all it means.'[9]

Desire and the Other

That all desire is 'the desire of the Other' is both a clinical observation and a theoretical point: clinically, it is observable that a patient will often experience desire as something that comes from 'out there' – it is something that 'happens' to one, that afflicts one, and is outside one's control, in much the same way as unconscious slips of the tongue or dreams seem to come from the Other, and are beyond one's control. Also, it is often noted that individuals come to desire what is desired by those around them; but in this observation, which involves small 'others', the Other is still written with a capital 'O', so it requires some explanation.

The first Other for the child is embodied by the mother; this one is the most important, as it is from this Other that the child acquires language, and contained within the signifiers that are passed from this Other to the child is the desire of the mother, which has in itself been created by the signifiers and their significations she inherited. In Lacan's words, 'primary identification ... occurs on the basis of the mother's omnipotence [and] makes the satisfaction of needs dependent upon the signifying apparatus, [which] also fragments, filters and models those needs in the defiles of the signifier's structure'.[10] In this way, the desire of the mother – here the representative of the Other – structures the desire of the child subject.

The primordial relationship of the baby with its mother is one of helpless dependency upon an omnipotent and unpredictable Other; and what if the Other chooses, for mysterious reasons, not to respond to the baby's demand – as in fact, mothers often do? The result is anxiety, which Lacan suggests is the other side of desire; it is, perhaps, even the seed-germ of desire:

> Desire begins to take shape in the margin in which demand is torn from need, this margin being the one that demand – whose appeal can be unconditional only with respect to the Other – opens up in the guise of the possible gap need may give rise to here, because it has no universal satisfaction (this is called 'anxiety'). A margin which, as linear as it may be, allows its vertiginous character to appear, provided it is not trampled by the elephantine feet of the Other's whimsy.[11]

This is where Lacan suggests that the acceptance of the Name-of-the-Father as representing the Law is a shield against the 'whimsy' of the Other, who must also submit to it; indeed, the Law originates in desire, which becomes '*raised to an absolute condition*' in this relationship of dependency. By this he means that the two-faced Janus of desire/anxiety that is part of the condition of the child's dependency becomes a condition in its own right, and that the signifiers in which it is held are repressed into the unconscious:

> representation's representative [a signifier] in the absolute condition is in its proper place in the unconscious, where it causes desire in accordance with the structure of fantasy I will extract from it. For it is clear here that man's continued ignorance of his desire is not so much ignorance of what he demands, which may after all be isolated, as ignorance of what his desire arises from.[12]

The connection between anxiety and desire is one of the central structuring forces in the Subject, and is also the reason Lacan postulates that the object cause of desire is also the object of anxiety.

Lacan talked a lot about the authenticity of desire, which he held to be the driving force for creativity: in the properly castrated subject, 'the true function of the Father ... is to unite desire with the Law, not to oppose it'.[13] But the formulation that 'desire is the desire of the Other' seems to deny the possibility of authenticity: it seems to suggest a permanent dependency of the Subject upon someone else for desire. This is not so, but needs a little further explanation.

The mother is not the only embodiment of the Other for the child (indeed, if she remains this way, the result is psychosis, as we have already seen). The Other – the symbolised mental universe – is different for everyone: every small other has an Other. The child soon comes into contact with other Others – that of its father and a little later, those of its peers. With each new Other that is encountered, the desire of this Other is transmitted in language; thus, as she/he grows up, the individual's desire becomes moulded by the desires of the many Others the Subject has identified with. Lacan suggests that in these secondary identifications, the 'influence' exerted by the others upon the Subject is that of a *structuring* (or restructuring) *of desire*, which passes through the medium of signifiers: 'It does not involve the assumption by the subject of the other's insignia, but rather the condition that the subject find the constitutive structure of his desire in the same gap opened up by the effect of signifiers in those who come to represent the Other for him, insofar as his demand is subjected to them.'[14] The individual Subject is thus formed by the complex interplay of many different identifications, as well as other environmental factors; so too is its desire.

8
That obscure object of desire
L'objet petit a

> Desire links Being to Non-Being. Thought gives rise to desire.
>
> (The Rig Veda)

L'objet petit a – the object cause of desire

One of Lacan's most famous concepts is that of *l'objet petit a* – translated in English as 'small a object' despite the fact that the 'a' in question represents the French word '*autre*', which in English would be 'other', so that perhaps 'small o object' would be more correct. However, too many writers have used 'small a object' for this change to be made now, and this text will use the French term, *l'objet petit a*, which has the advantage of maintaining the link with the idea of *le petit autre*. The main importance of it, whatever it is called, is that it is the object cause of desire.

For the genesis of the term *l'objet petit a*, we must return to the Mirror Stage. The *petit a* (*petit autre*) is the 'small other', the image the baby recognises as its own in the mirror and with which it forms a powerful relationship of identification. Lacan first mentions the *petit a* in a seminar in 1955, and places it in the Imaginary realm – the part of the psyche which holds the child's sensuous, self-centred fantasies of the world. In its identification with other human beings, many 'small others' come into being in the child's world, and become the objects onto which all kinds of ideas and fantasies may be affixed. There is from here a small step to be made from the small other to 'small other objects'.

In a seminar in 1957, the *objet petit a* begins to take on the meaning of the object of desire, which means not this or that specific object that you think you desire, but what is aimed at or sought after that seems to be *contained within* a particular object – for convenience, one may begin to think of it as the 'desirable quality' of the object, or *what is desirable in* the real-world object.

'The object of desire in the usual sense is either a fantasy which supports the desire, or a lure.'[1] Lacan specifies here that the *objet petit a* is the 'imaginary cause of desire' rather than 'what the desire tends towards', to emphasise that this is not a 'real-world object' (a thing), but an object in the sense of 'object relations' – that is, the vehicle upon which a function is exercised (the breast, the stool, the genitalia), and whose relational properties (e.g. controllability for the stool, excitability for the genitalia) form the basis of the different kinds of relationship one may have with the exterior world.

Lacan never suggested that the *objet petit a* was derived from part objects, only that real-world objects which have *something of the properties* of part objects are often the 'receptacles' for the *objet petit a*. For example, money shares the property of the stool (the object of the anal function) in being something that may be lost or retained, the unexpected loss of which may be a cause of anxiety, the 'spending' of which may be a cause of enjoyment in its own right (how common is the phenomenon of 'spending money for its own sake'?), and the giving and retention of which both have meaning for other people. In other words, it is not money in itself that is an object cause of desire, but its stool-like properties make it a very good receptacle for the object cause of desire.

The *objets petit a* may be seen as a fragment of the Phallus, which arises from castration, when the child understands that the Phallus is possessed neither by itself nor its father, nor yet any living person. However, the lost Phallus cannot be forgotten – the Subject knows it must have existed from the fact that it has lost it. The Phallus leaves traces of itself everywhere – a little like the mirror of the Snow Queen in the fairy tale, which breaks into a thousand pieces that lodge themselves in objects and people. These Phallic fragments are the *objet petit a* – the object cause of desire – and can be found in many things: fast cars, the latest technological gadget, the 'perfect' cocktail dress ... and in other people – a woman who hankers after the love of a powerful man may well be attracted to the Phallic fragment he appears to possess. This versatility of representation is conferred by the signifier to which the Phallus is attached in the paternal metaphor, which can be substituted for others.

Furthermore, because the desire of the child is to have the Phallus *for the mother*, so in later life, this desire may be transformed into the desire either to have it sometimes for its own sake, or to be the possessor of it for a new beloved object. The dynamics of this new relationship will therefore depend upon the beloved object also being castrated, and desiring the Phallus, which the Subject seeks to possess in order to 'win' her/him. (As you will see in the next chapter, it is usually but not exclusively the man who tries to be the Phallus bearer for the woman, whose role is to want to believe that he may have it.) The quest to possess the Phallic fragment is a well-spring of creativity and effort: the search for the solution to the insoluble maths problem, to invent a new chess strategy, to perfect your skill at the piano, to discover the structure of DNA ... The pursuit of the Phallus is qualitatively different from the pursuit of fame or social recognition, as it is object-focused (or objec*tive*-focused) rather than purely narcissistic (although there will necessarily be a narcissistic element in everything we do); it is to do with the attempt to incorporate in oneself the Phallic fragment.

In a seminar in 1960–61, Lacan formulated a metaphor to explain the *objet petit a* in its relation with real-world objects; he used the term *agalma*, drawn from Plato's *Symposium*, which in Greek means ornament or offering to the gods. The *agalma* is contained inside a box which itself is of no value. Thus, the *objet petit a* is the *agalma* – the precious thing – inside a box which may have many forms, none of which is very important. Lacan comes to the idea of the *agalma* by way of his interest in the desire exhibited by Alcibiades in Plato's text.

In the *Symposium*, Alcibiades describes how he, as a beautiful youth, tried to seduce Socrates, despite the old man's ugliness, because he had seen the 'divine and golden images of such fascinating beauty' within him.[2] All the properties of goodness, courage, and wisdom were contained within the unlikely receptacle of the Silenus-like old Socrates – a receptacle of no value, and indeed the object of Alcibiades' mockery. In the *Symposium*, Socrates never yields to the temptations of Alcibiades, who, 'by exhibiting his own object as castrated, flaunts the fact that he is imbued with desire ... for someone else who is present, Agathon'.[3] In this Platonic story, therefore, are the fundamentals of the dynamics of desire: its ultimate but unattainable object is the *agalma* within Socrates, its subject is the castrated (symbolically – wanting, drunken, and demanding) Alcibiades, who uses as a lure for a secondary object of desire (Agathon) his own desire or neediness, which he knows makes him desirable. This last point is not negligible.

As mentioned a little earlier, sexual and love relationships depend upon a dynamic in which the object of desire must be in search of the Phallus in the Subject (or the other way around – the Subject must want to believe the love-object has the Phallus and must, like Alcibiades, flaunt its castratedness as a lure for it). It is only too common to observe the attractiveness that helplessness in a woman has for a would-be prince (*'I'm so bad at maths!'* is a common cry of the siren), whom she allows to play the part of the Phallus bearer (*'James is so good with business plans – I just leave it all to him'*); or the other way around – Lacan pointed out that these are roles of choice and not biological determination. On a more obvious sexual level, most pornographic (and sub-pornographic – increasingly common in everyday life) images are based upon the presentation of a woman *not as a plastically beautiful object* but as a Subject in a state of desire for the literal and Freudian phallus: it is her imagined desire (and her desire to be desired in an endless game of mirrors) that causes desire.

On a more general note, because it is the root of creation, desire is desirable in itself, and is cherished by its Subject. All writers, musicians, and artists harbour a deep fear of losing desire, for they know that with it will go their creativity. As Oscar Wilde said: 'In this world, there are only two tragedies: one is not getting what one wants; the other is getting it.' The resistance of patients in analysis to being cured is, Lacan says, usually nothing more (or less) than the desire to sustain desire. Desire has been involved in the foundation of the Subject, and is also the guiding hand in the inscription of the symptom, and the *sinthome* within it; the fear of losing one's desire is, for Lacan, utterly reasonable and not to be discounted when one undertakes an analysis.

Desire is a structuring force within the Subject

The first receptacle (or representation) for the Phallus was the Name-of-the-Father; or if we return to our algebraic form, the Phallus was first hidden beneath the signifier of the Name-of-the-Father. In addition, the Phallus, being a signified, itself had a signifier which has been repressed. But signifiers are subject to substitution, so let us make one:

$$\frac{\text{Name of the Father}}{\text{Phallus}} \rightarrow \frac{\text{S1 [a master signifier]}}{a}$$

The object cause of desire replaces the Phallus beneath the bar: the representatives of the signified desire have changed, even though the desire remains the same. Above the bar of metaphor, the Name-of-the-Father is replaced by a master signifier. Remember, because this is a metaphorical structure in which a signifier has been expelled, there is still this 'lost' and 'unstable' signifier in the unconscious – the never-quite-determined representation of the Phallus: this is what gives the *objet petit a* its elusive quality. The Name-of-the-Father is an object of identification for the Subject, as well as the representative of the Other: it is central to the construction of both Subject and its ego. It is the signifier that the Subject *can* enunciate as representing the object of desire; the master signifiers that take its place will have exactly the same character. This is why Lacan attributes such an important structural role to the master signifiers as being the backbone upon which the Subject is built. Consider the following example:

A man loves sailing and has built much of his image and identity around this; many of his desires revolve around the sea and sailing and the sort of society that goes with it – all this is observable in his choices of clothes, homes, women, etc. 'Sailing' is among his master signifiers. In his early life, this man's father was a keen sailor, and in his identification with his father and fierce rivalry with his brothers for his father's attention, the boy's skill at the helm became his main 'weapon' of power – his representation of the Phallus (or objet petit a). If you think of how the Name-of-the-Father hides the true object of the mother's desire (who was, after all a seaman), one can easily see how 'sailing' has replaced the Name-of-the-Father as the metaphorical representation of the object of desire.

Desire exists in tension with anxiety, and the ultimate object of desire and power exists in tension with the ultimate anxiety-creating lack of it (which could be experienced as total helplessness in the face of incomprehensible persecution). We could postulate that they fit like lock and key in this formulation:

object cause of desire → lack-cause-of-anxiety

Just as the primordial desirable object is the Phallus, the primordial lack that causes anxiety could be seen as the castration.[4] Lacan represents the castrated subject as $\mathbf{S}$ (sometimes referred to as the barred Subject); in the way in which it is used, $\mathbf{S}$ can be thought of as signifying the castrated*ness* of the Subject.

I mentioned in chapter 3 that master signifiers exist in negative and positive forms (like a photograph) – for every master signifier that is articulated by the Subject, there is its negative match that is repressed; likewise for what happens beneath the signifiers' bars in this formulation, which is my own:

Unconscious		Spoken
$\dfrac{\text{S2}}{\mathbf{S}}$	$\leftarrow\rightarrow$	$\dfrac{\text{S1}}{a}$

Just as there is a tension between the signifiers S1 and S2, there is the same between the repressed signifiers associated with the object cause of desire and the lack-cause-of-anxiety. If we return to the little girl whose master signifiers included 'lucky', we can see that the repressed signifier was 'unlucky' and where her object cause of desire was to be lucky, her anxiety was that she wasn't. Of course, I am over-simplifying enormously, as this explanation takes no account of the repressed 'unstable' signifiers: in reality, 'lucky' was a master signifier that was closely linked in a signifying chain with 'best' (as in '*I'm so lucky, we always go to the best place on holiday – Cornwall*', etc.). It is the job of analysis to trace these signifier chains – 'best' was the tip of the iceberg whose hidden part was 'second best', which is what the girl felt in relation to her brother. Her *objet petit a* – associated with being 'the best' at everything and having 'the best' of everything – was pursued in opposition to her anxiety about being second best – not as good.

It is around these master signifiers that the Subject is constructed, and one can see, if one takes Lacan's view that the ego is the fiction you tell yourself about yourself, the structural role played in the building of the ego by the relationship between the object cause of desire and the master signifiers. The little girl's ego identity was that of excellence – *competitive* excellence rather than excellence for its own sake. Her competitiveness in all things was remarked by teachers and family members alike; she fluctuated in temper between cheerful – sometimes manic – optimism and outbursts of rage; and if she couldn't be 'the best' at something, she would derogate it as not being worthwhile.

Just as the master signifiers are substitutes for the Name-of-the-Father, the object cause of desire replaces the lost Phallus as the only thing that can answer the subject's lack that causes anxiety. I hope this final example will show clearly the relationship between these elements:

A woman in her forties suffered chronic insomnia, caused by her inability to stop thinking, or to 'switch off her mind'. She was a mathematician by career, and her master signifiers included 'rationality' and 'logic': she was almost exasperatingly rational. Beneath the bar of her master signifiers was hidden her great desire for a rational universe, for achievable solutions to problems; the Phallic enjoyment of her life revolved around this. Analysis revealed a childhood in which she had suffered greatly from a mother whose apparently illogical decisions had cost the family greatly and whose 'childish irrationality' was a great source of suffering and anger to the child, who proceeded to build her own personality around the signifier and the objects that she felt were her best defence. Beneath the bar of 'irrationality' in her unconscious was, as ever, the anxiety of the helplessness – castratedness – she had experienced as a result of it as child. Because there is *jouissance* in the functioning of the psychological apparatus, part of the woman's problem was that she enjoyed thinking too much (in her insomniac moments, she would solve chess problems in her mind). The defence mechanism she had developed in childhood against the anxiety caused by her helplessness against irrationality had got out of control: her *jouissance* was transgressing both the

pleasure and the reality principles. The insomnia became particularly bad whenever situations arose that caused her to re-
experience castration anxiety: difficulties at work that she could
not 'solve' however much she thought would cause her
completely sleepless nights, resulting in exhaustion and a vicious
circle of not being able to think clearly, and feeling even more
anxious about this.

In chapter 12, I shall discuss how Lacanian analysis deals with
this system of anxiety/desire/signifiers/Subject.

The Thing

Desire is also associated with a manifestation which may largely
belong to the Real – the Thing (*das Ding*), which is also beyond
representation – but not in the same way as it is with the *objet
petit a* or the Phallus. The Thing attracts desire perhaps because
it is the object of loss itself: the unsymbolisable and unimaginable reality of loss. 'In reality, desire through the object … [is
only] the Thing, of which he neither has nor ever will have any
representation, which is not a goal because it will never be
reached, but around which all our representations, all our affects
never stop gravitating.'[5]

Das Ding is a formulation of Freud's to describe what is
'characterised by the fact that it is impossible for us to imagine',
but it is also mainly characterised by its absence. In 1895, Freud
suggested that a part of the neuropsychic apparatus was shared by
a configuration of neurones carrying the memories of an object
and a configuration invested by current perceptions of that
object; he suggested that *das Ding* was produced by the inconsistencies between the two. The Thing is therefore what
produces that feeling of '*This is not how I remembered it to be –
something is irretrievably lost but I could not possibly say what it is*.'
The main property of the Thing is to be lost.

In bringing the Thing into Lacanian theory, we have to return to Lacan's attempts to reconcile some Freudian formulations with his own. Freud made a distinction between *Wortvorstellungen*, word-presentations, and *Sachvorstellungen*, thing-presentations; both are bound together in his preconscious–conscious system, whereas in Freud's idea of the unconscious, only thing-presentations are found. However, Lacan points out that this is not a contradiction of his own conviction that the unconscious is made up of signifiers, because there are two words in German for 'thing' – *das Ding* and *die Sache*. *Die Sache* is the symbolic representation of a thing, whereas *das Ding* is the thing in the real, which is 'the beyond-of-the-signified'. Therefore, the *Sachvorstellungen* or thing-presentations in Freud's conception of the unconscious may be equated with signifiers, as opposed to *das Ding*, which is outside language and the unconscious.

Freud's Thing is the object of yearning, of desire; it creates *jouissance*, and is the object of language, while being unsymbolisable. We seek to approach it all the time in what we say, but we can only circle it. Freud held that the Thing was the 'sovereign good' to which subjects aspire, but which is always unattainable, because attaining it would transgress the reality principle and will be experienced as suffering or evil.[6] In the end, therefore, Freud concluded that there was no 'sovereign good', because attaining it would be the ultimate evil.

Lacan's innovation was to equate the Thing with the mother – not the real mother, obviously, but the mother-who-is-lost: the absence of mother. 'It is as a function of this beyond-of-the-signified [the Thing] and of an emotional relationship to it that the subject keeps its distance and is constituted in a kind of relationship characterised by primary affect, prior to any repression.'[7] Lacan implies here that the Subject is constituted by its separation from and emotional relationship with the Thing, which is unsymbolisable and therefore cannot be repressed.

This relationship with the Thing is so charged with the primary affects characteristic of the mother–baby relationship that he goes on: 'the whole development of the mother/child inter-psychology – and that is badly expressed in the so-called categories of frustration, satisfaction and dependence – is nothing more than an immense development of the essential character of the maternal thing, of the mother, insofar as she occupies the place of the Thing'.[8] The obvious value of study-ing the matter by focusing on the Thing aspect of the mother rather than any real mothers is that in the absence of real mothers, the Thing, as an imaginary object, persists in the Subject's psyche, and will continue to operate in its own right.

> The Thing is that which in the Real, the primordial real ...
> suffers from the signifier – and you should understand that it is
> a Real that we do not yet have to limit, the Real in its totality,
> both the Real of the subject and the Real he has to deal with
> as exterior to him ... this Thing was there from the beginning
> ... it was the first thing that separated itself from everything the
> subject began to name and articulate.[9]

I would postulate that if a primary characteristic of the Thing is to be unsymbolised and unsymbolisable, then perhaps the Thing is what is lost at the point of birth: the environment *in utero*, a state in which the baby had no needs, because all its needs were being met by the functioning of the mother. At birth, the change in environment and the development of physical needs (to feed, to excrete) creates a situation in which the baby 'remembers' vaguely that there was another way of being, but nothing of it, for without anything to compare it with (in the absence of dialectical possibility) it could never be represented. The Thing is therefore by its nature only conceptualised after the event of its loss, and the lost object was never and could never be symbolised. It is thus a representation of an unrepre-sented object – a representation of pure loss.

Because the concept of the Thing is created by the polarities between presence and absence, it is outside the Symbolic but exists at the point at which the Imaginary touches the Real. Although the Thing has something of the effects of the *objet petit a*, or the Phallus, the distinction of its origins gives it a special flavour. Where the *objet petit a* arises from the Phallus, and thereby indirectly from the desire of the mother, the Thing arises from the primary affects of a relationship with what is not-yet-represented – the unforgettable-but-already-forgotten other. To return to a total enjoyment of this phantasmatic mother – this mother-as-world – would require a dismantling of the Subject – a kind of regression to a pre-language state that is simply impossible. Because the Subject is brought into being by signifiers, and the Thing exists outside the Symbolic realm, absolute *jouissance* in the Thing would require an exit from the realm of signifiers, which is the realm of subjectivity, and the Subject itself would be erased, annihilated. The other important thing in equating the Thing with the mother (even if it is the *absent* and impossible mother), is that this highlights its inaccessibility as an object of total *jouissance* because of the taboo of incest.

This conception of incest towards the mother makes it the most fundamental incest taboo – a point of difference between Lacan and Lévi-Strauss, who considered only the prohibition of incest with the father in the building of his structures of kinship. But for Lacan, the danger of incest with the mother is far greater: after all, what is the most intimate thing for a Subject, and yet the most threatening, in terms of its potential to block its access to the Symbolic? The mother is in many ways the gatekeeper of the Symbolic – it is her presence/absence that creates the polarities in which proto-thinking can begin, it is she who embodies the Other, and only she can invoke the Name-of-the-Father. Therefore, the mother – structurally inaccessible, signified as prohibited, and imagined by the baby Subject as the sovereign good – constitutes, in her absence and in the impossibility of fully accessing her, the Thing.

The Thing is therefore an object of transgression, which is observable in behaviours that begin as seeking *jouissance*, and end in self-destruction. The Thing may be thought of as the object of the death drive: those who seek oblivion in heroin or people who strangle themselves in the name of sexual excitement may be acting out their search for the Thing. The search for the Thing exists in tension with the pursuit of the Phallus, and of the *objet petit a*; this dynamic of tensions set up between the different objects can be seen as the sum of the forces of creativity.

Desire and the Borromean knot

The component that belongs in the Real is the drive, or drives, which were mentioned in chapter 6. It is important to make the point that the erotic drive and sexual desire are not the same thing; in common parlance (and sometimes even within psychoanalytic circles) they are often spoken of as if they were synonymous, or as if sexual desire was merely the erotic drive focused upon an object. While the latter statement is not untrue, sexual desire is also more than that, and the formulation itself begs the questions: *What object? And by what mechanism is the drive focused?*

At the very beginning of the infant's life, sexual desire does not exist – it can come into being only after the Subject's entry into the symbolic realm; at this point, any stirrings in the genitalia are merely an effect of a drive, in its Real state. Imagine a hypothetical human infant, isolated from all human society. In the unlikely event of its surviving, the manifestation of the erotic drive in its genitalia can be answered by masturbation, but it would be masturbation without any link to arousing imaginings: a purely physical response devoid of fantasy – perhaps not even a very pleasurable act. That would be a response to the erotic drive that is devoid of sexual desire; it is outside human society and is *entirely hypothetical*: even severely mentally disturbed children would not function in this way, as they are likely to have entered in some degree into the Imaginary realm.

The child's Imaginary realm develops almost as soon as it is born. It is linked closely with the sensuous world of the mother, at first by means of the breast and other part objects. For the sake of convenience, let us here think of the Imaginary as a primordial perception-based conception of Otherness. The infant that is at the stage of *l'Autre jouissance* develops object relations in its Imaginary realm: its hypotheses at this point are entirely self-centred, but it is able to link sensation with exterior objects and to begin to form hypotheses about these objects. At this point, the erotic drive as experienced in its genitalia comes to be associated with the enjoyment of something exterior to self: the infant recognises that the gratification comes from a relationship with another object, although the source of the arousal is still a purely internal drive. It is at this point, therefore, that the foundation for desire is laid – for without the recognition of objects and their potential for giving pleasure or causing frustration, there can be neither anxiety nor desire.

The final thread – the Symbolic – comes with the child's entry into language – as it gradually becomes a 'speaking being', functioning within human society. Once the child enters into the symbolic realm by means of the discourse of the Other, erotic arousal (*but not yet desire*) will become *attached to other human figures by means of speech*. However, desire is created by the *failure of the Other to fully and satisfactorily symbolise the erotic need*. As you will remember, the essential property of the Real is that is cannot be symbolised – it will always elude language or any other form of representation.

We have now, in the knot of the Symbolic, Imaginary, and Real, the mould in which desire is cast: in the impossibility of the Other (on the thread of the Symbolic) to symbolise the drive (on the thread of the Real), tied into the fantasies built up in object relations of the Imaginary (which for the most part are buried in the unconscious, but which, given enough time on the analyst's couch, may emerge as a signifying chain). The object cause of desire, arising as it does from the acceptance of the paternal metaphor (castration), may be located at the point of contact between the three threads.

The mathematics of desire

As the cause of desire the *objet petit a* appears in the formula of fantasy:

$\$ \Diamond a$

This shows the relationship between the subject of the unconscious, divided by its entry into the universe of signifiers and the *objet petit a*, the unconscious cause of its desire. The slash on the S represents the division of the Subject caused by its entry into language. The *objet petit a* is shown as something lost, an empty place, a gap that the Subject will try to plug all its life with various imaginary objects determined by the Subject's history, and in particular its encounters with the signifiers and fantasies of others. The lozenge shape represents the fantasmatic relationship of the barred Subject with its *objet petit a*.

Lacan used the topology of the 'torus' – the rubber tubing inside a tyre – to explain the chaining of desire to the desire of the Other (see Figure 2).

If you look at Figure 3 below, the desire of the Subject (the child) is like the ring on its side that circles around the desire of the mother (the ring lying flat), which in itself circles around something entirely elsewhere (the hollow centre of the ring lying flat). The desire of the child is produced by the gap between the demand it makes upon the mother for love, which

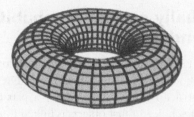

Figure 2 A torus

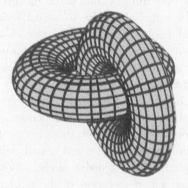

Figure 3 Two interlocking toruses

appears like a cut on the plane of the ring representing the child, and what the mother actually wants, which is in the hole. You then have to think of this torus, which symbolises the relationship between the desire of the Subject (child) and the desire of the mother, as tied to the torus of the desire of the Other in this way.

Therefore the desire of the Subject circles, without knowing it, the desire of the Other, by means of its circling what it thinks is the desire of the mother. In this way, what the Subject desires is the desire of the Other.

The mutually exclusive cohabitation of love and desire

When Freud talks about choice of object or love object, it's generally a whole person. But when he studies the object at which the partial drives aim, it is usually a part object (breast, food, etc.). The choice of first objects is linked to experiences of satisfaction obtained through dependency. Later, after puberty, the Subject is faced with new possibilities and chooses new external objects built on the model of its first objects, but moving from the initial affectivity to sexual sensuality. Freud pointed out the difficulty of making these two radically different domains (affectivity/sensuality) cohabit harmoniously. It seemed to him that human beings are unable to completely love what they desire and to desire what they love.

It was in examining this disharmony that Lacan described the relationship between need, desire, and demand, and focused most closely upon desire. However, there is – as interestingly – an undeniable link between love and sexual desire: the most diehard Casanova (male or female) might admit to being in constant search of a perfect fusion of the two; and the most cynical people, who insist they would never mix up love and lust, do find themselves vulnerable to 'sentimental' emotions. It should not be forgotten that in some societies which do not have much of a romantic tradition and in which marriage is a social transaction, heterosexual love can be *less* socially acceptable than sexual desire.

The ease with which the desire for love and sexual desire become intertwined and the possibilities for misunderstandings to arise are encapsulated in the very genesis of both things. The demands possible in both cases are almost bound to create confusion – the first, because it can only be answered in the fulfilment of the 'extra' of the demand (the effort put into making a really good meal, rather than just one that will quell hunger), and the second because as there is no justifiable need attached to the demand – why should it be answered, except as a proof of love? It is not uncommon that it is the 'giver' of the sexual favour who is in search of love rather than the recipient, and unless there is perfectly matched lust on both sides, there is almost bound to be disappointment; and even in cases of perfectly matched lust, there is room for confusion further down the line because what is 'given' so closely resembles a proof of love.

A Modern Lacanian view may be that the discrepancy between love and desire may be examined in terms of their origins in drives. Love is probably linked closely with the drive for self-preservation and the erotic drive, while desire may be linked with the erotic drive and the death drive (as manifested in the pursuit of *jouissance*). There is therefore an overlap (in the field of the erotic) but also never a complete match. The genesis of this mismatch is different for boys and girls, because of their different responses to the process of castration.

9

Gender bending
The formula of 'sexuation'

La Femme n'existe pas

For Lacan, it is not the biological reality of sex that determines our gender identity; he saw gender as the result of an identification process, and of a process he calls 'sexuation'. This has to do with how a Subject determines itself in relationship with the Phallus and castration. In this, Lacan adopts a very different position from Freud, who based his view of the Oedipus complex on a biological difference between boys and girls and the presence or absence of a penis, taking the threat of castration very literally – a position for which he has been much criticised. For Lacan, castration is the symbolic loss of an imaginary object – the Phallus – which is the object of the mother's desire; both boys and girls have to submit to the paternal metaphor, which involves the acceptance that they haven't got the Phallus.

Because of the prematurity of the human infant, the baby is impotent and unable to oppose the mother in the pursuit of her desire; not to submit to the paternal metaphor would expose the child to depression and collapse, because there is nothing it can do to impose its own will against its mother's. In a sense, the paternal metaphor is a '*marché de dupes*' – a game of complicity in a lie – which saves the child from a position of total despair. However, the attitude taken by the child, boy or girl, towards this symbolic castration may differ. The boy, in renouncing the idea of being the Phallus for the mother, may identify with the father in the expectation of becoming one day the bearer of an object that would satisfy a loved one; the boy's 'quest' is for some Phallic fragments. The girl, in renouncing the idea that she has the Phallus, may adopt the same position as the boy, but she also has an alternative: because as she is of the same kind as the mother, she can continue to identify with the mother. She knows that one day, she will be the mother – she will inherit the mother's mantle, *including the mother's desire for the Phallus*, which will be brought to her by someone else. The girl therefore does not need to try to possess the Phallus in order to please someone else: she may choose to try instead to become the object of desire of the father, as the representative of the Phallus through the paternal metaphor, and may enter into a rivalry with the mother vis-à-vis the Phallus. The girl's position after castration is therefore not of wanting to possess the Phallus (or fragments thereof) but to attract someone who appears to have it.

There is another dimension to this process, which is highly anxiogenic for the boy but very much less so for the girl. The infant's primary identification is with the mother, and the Otherly enjoyment experienced in its early life owes greatly to the sense of omnipotence that comes with this identification as well as a freedom to enjoy her body as if it were one's own. At castration, not only does the boy realise that he hasn't got the Phallus, he also understands that he can no longer identify with the mother but must find some new kind of identity. The girl, on the other hand, remains identified with the mother, and so may remain in some reduced form of Otherly enjoyment.

Another way in which castration is more terrifying to the boy is that it excludes him from the dualistic relationship between the mother and the Phallus. He can witness how she goes about the pursuit of her desires, but not only does he have to accept that none of it has anything to do with him, it also makes no sense for him to follow suit in some continuance of identification, because he will never be a mother like her: he is truly shut out. The girl, on the other hand, in the comforting knowledge that she is her mother's rightful successor, can remain within the mother–Phallus relationship; she can follow where mother leads, adopting the same strategies in pursuit of satisfaction, knowing that one day she will be the mother. The boy, in order to reclaim some relationship with the Phallus and not succumb to the helpless depression of castration anxiety, must seek it for himself, by engaging with the Other, and if he is allowed, he may begin by identifying with the father, who is after all the first Phallus-bearer. The girl may also do this, but has a choice in the position she takes, whereas there is only one truly successful position towards castration that can be taken by the boy.

There are perhaps only two things biologically 'inherent' in the positions taken by the boy or the girl towards castration: the first is the fact that the girl can become the mother, where the boy cannot; the second is the fact that the boy can commit incest with the mother, where the girl cannot.

Lacan suggested four 'mathemes' for sexuation; two which define the masculine identity and two which define the feminine, in the context of their being 'speaking beings'; but any speaking being has the possibility of being in one group or the other. This supports the common observation that masculine and feminine identities are not dependent on biological sex.

The two statements that Lacan makes about male sexual identity are:

- All men are subject to the Phallic function.
- There is at least one man that is an exception to the Phallic function.

The Phallic function, first of all, refers to castration – but also to everything that follows on from it: to the fact that once you have accepted that you have not got the Phallus, but that it is somewhere in existence, then it becomes *the* object to be sought after. The second statement refers to the hypothetical existence of a father who has the Phallus and who therefore has not been subject to castration, in the sense that in order for an idea to exist, its converse must also exist. This is what Freud described in his myth of the pride of the primitive horde – that in prehistoric cultures, the father of the group had all the women, and the children were either killed or expelled. This mythical father prevents the boy children from accessing Society, and at some point, the children kill him.

The hypothesis of the Phallus-bearer is necessary to allow the existence of male identity in the same way that a class of objects is constituted by the possibility of the absence of the traits that distinguish it. In other words, if there is a class of creatures with two legs, then there must be other creatures with more or fewer legs. This means that boys hypothesise that they are the heirs of this mythical father, but they are not. Men constitute an ensemble which is the universal ensemble of all those who have submitted to castration; they fantasise that an absolute enjoyment of the Perfect Object was experienced by this mythical father – but that this *jouissance* is inaccessible and forbidden for the common man. However, masculine *jouissance* must be Phallic (object-focused) and delimited by castration, which means that objects can be enjoyed only within the laws of Society. As the universal ensemble, it is typically a masculine function to form groups such as armies, football teams, churches, etc. – which have a Phallic function, in that they are formed in the pursuit of an objective.

Lacan's statements to describe the feminine position are:

- Not all women are subject to the Phallic function.
- There is no exception to castration.

This paradox means that while the feminine identity is also constituted by castration, girls do not have to seek to possess the Phallus (and therefore enter completely into object-focused enjoyment), as they have the option of adopting the mother's desire as their own. According to Lacan, this means that the girl does not have to accept the complete loss of the mythical object; I would prefer to say that she is not completely excluded from the relationship between the mother and the Phallus.

Imagine the situation of the boy after castration, when he has accepted that the Phallus-bearer is something/someone else: what then is *he* in relation to the mother, whose desire is the Phallus? He seems to be thrown out of the relationship entirely, while the girl at least knows that she will one day become mother, and attract the Phallus-bearer. The position of the boy is one that must create anxiety and a vast sense of loss of identity – or rather, he must find other ways of establishing his identity, outside of his relationship with his mother. After his expulsion from the fantasised relationship with the mother's desire, the boy can only hope, by means of identification with the father and by means of Phallic functioning, at some point to become a Phallus-bearer too; and as the Phallus is an imaginary object, he must seek it in all his object relations. This accounts for the great variety and randomness in so much masculine activity and inventiveness – boys must find a place and a meaning for themselves, following the lure of the Phallus, and almost every square inch of the field of human life may be explored in this pursuit. Boys seek to identify themselves in what they do, while girls tend to identify themselves by what they are. However, one can only say 'tend to' about girls, because, according to Lacan, it is impossible to generalise about women, because '*La Femme n'existe pas.*'

Consider the vast combination of possibilities for the girl in the position she chooses to adopt in relation to her castration: she may take on elements of the Phallic function, and elements of the mother's desire, with each individual mixing and match- ing the degree of the one or the other, or moving between them, so that at the end of the day, there is no one single feminine solution to the issue of castration. This is why Lacan insisted that 'there is no such thing as The Woman, with "the" defining it as a universal group, because in its essence, she is not all'.[1] For him, there are only individual women – all of them constituted differently by their different responses to castration. Man however – a universal Man – does exist, because he is the product of a path that is rigidly set by his biology and position in castration, and there is little variance or deviation from this path. The boy who tries to adopt the girl's position of adopting the mother's desire as his own becomes faintly ridiculous, and has to play a great mental trick upon himself in order to maintain this position.

The second biological determinant of gender identity is, as mentioned above, that incest with the mother is possible for boys but not for girls. The prohibition of incest is not logically inscribed in the structure of the Subject in the same way for men and for women. For Lacan, the fundamental incest is between boys and their mothers, and castration therefore has the additional consequence for them of acting to prohibit this incest, in that in accepting the Name-of-the-Father, the boy has accepted that, he will not be able to satisfy his mother's desire.

'There is no such thing as sexual rapports'

This is another of Lacan's deliberately provocative statements, by which he sought to make his audience think about the true nature of things. In using the word 'rapports' rather than relations, he underlined the fantasmatic quality of the relationship between individuals engaged in a sexual act: he was not saying that sexual relations don't exist, but that those relations do not have a character of mutual understanding, agreement, or *rapports*. The individual man and the individual woman in a joint sexual act is each pursuing a form of enjoyment that is distinct from and irrelevant to the other's: the object of the man is different from the object of the woman.

It is a commonplace to say that men are goal-orientated in their attitude towards sex; a more psychoanalytic way of putting it would be that, being subject to the Phallic function, their enjoyment or *jouissance* comes from their focus upon an object in sex, as in other things. With women – as in all things – there are many different possible ways, and many sources of enjoyment or *jouissance*, including that of being the object of her partner's Phallic functioning.

10

Four Discourses
Four forms of relationship

The Four Discourses appear in Lacan's Seminar XVII, in 1969; they are his attempt to formalise what he had observed of the different ways in which people relate to each other, and of the economy of knowledge and enjoyment (*jouissance*) in social relationships. The term 'discourse' relates to the organisation of communication between a Subject and an other; the four 'others' that Lacan has chosen to focus upon are the Master, the University, the Analyst, and the Hysteric. Lacan drew his formulations from his real-life observations of masters (people in positions of power), universities, psychoanalysts, and hysterical patients; however, his formalisations of their relationships with the Subject could be far more widely applied. The Master could represent anyone in a position of power; the University could represent any institution, whether academic, corporate, govern-mental, or commercial; the Analyst may be the person with whom the Subject has a relationship which allows and elicits disclosures that move the Subject towards a deeper personal insight; the Hysteric is the person who asks questions about exterior matters out of a position of genuine need and interest, and who thereby forces the Subject to elucidate matters as if it were the Master. Also, these four 'positions' within the Discourses are not rigidly specific to their titles: anyone can and may find themselves, at various points in their lives, in the position of either the speaker or the receiver of any of the Discourses. The humblest worker will at some point be the Master to someone else; you do not need to be at a university to experience the relationship between an institution and someone anxious to attain the status guaranteed by it; and the Hysteric's discourse is, as we shall see, one that we all have to adopt if we are ever to learn anything.

A Subject's style of communication reveals its relationship with signifiers and its *objet petit a*; the Subject's structure determines the manner in which it engages in social interactions. These four discourses illustrate several forms of intersubjective relations; they can be seen as a form of clinical description based not on symptoms but on the structure that underlies symptoms. The Discourses are forms of social interaction in which anybody might participate and do not necessarily have to be uttered by flesh-and-blood people. Examples of discourses that do not depend on articulation by real people would be the World War I posters of Lord Kitchener saying, 'Your country needs You!'; or advertising slogans, which make use of a plethora of different positions – sometimes the Master, sometimes the University, sometimes even the Hysteric, in an attempt to persuade by seduction.

Lacan's Discourses are formulated into mathemes, inspired by Hegel's discourse between master and slave; his other main influence here was Marxist economics (perhaps fuelled by the revolutionary atmosphere of France in the late 1960s). Hegel's Master–Slave dialectic is a story he created as an attempt to describe and explain the formation of human consciousness out of a dialectic of interpersonal relations. He suggests that when two individuals meet, they feel challenged by the differences in the other, and that this 'threat' to their sense of self is resolved in a struggle that results in one assuming the role of Master, and the other of Slave. These newly defined identities then deal with reality in different ways: the Slave has to learn about it in order to serve the Master and to preserve him/herself as a useful person, while the Master has only to maintain his/her relationship of superiority over the Slave to ensure his/her survival, but by the same token becomes increasingly helpless in dealing with the exterior world. Lacan married this Hegelian myth with the idea of 'surplus value' drawn from Marxist economics – the value added to any raw produce as a result of the labour and knowledge of the workers.

Lacan equated the object cause of desire (*l'objet petit a*) with surplus value: like the *objet petit a*, surplus value is the thing constantly sought after which no one can actually have and enjoy; the workers produce it by their labour, but must give it up to the capitalist, and the capitalist can't fully enjoy it either, because she/he is obliged always to reinvest it. To take the analogy further than this is not particularly fruitful, but what is interesting is that Lacan's interest in economic relationships allowed him to formulate a matheme to show the relationship between four elements: the agent, the truth, the other, and production (what is produced by the relationship). This is a particularly efficient way of showing what is the result – the *product* – of a discourse.

agent	the other
truth	production

The 'agent' in this matheme is the Subject – the 'giver' of the discourse; the 'other' is the one to whom discourse is addressed, even if that other is not one particular person. The agent also need not be a real person but something represented by a person, or an institution as embodied in a person or people. Under the message of the agent is hidden the truth, which is masked by the official statement; and hidden under the other is 'production' – what the agent (or Subject) finally gets out of the relationship. In his first formulation – based upon Hegel's Master–Slave discourse – the production was the surplus value produced by the ability of the slave, which Lacan equates with object cause of desire; however, as we shall see in the other Discourses, other kinds of production are the result of different relationships. Lacan then substituted into this basic matheme the four elements, S1, S2, $, and a, according to the kind of discourse he is describing.

S1 is a signifier that represents the Subject in its relationship with all other signifiers – the 'master signifier'. Remember that the master signifiers may be thought of as the signifiers that best define the Subject – they have a central place, like a skeleton, around which the Subject has been constructed. One could imagine, for example, master signifiers for Julius Caesar being 'Rome', 'civilisation', 'discipline', 'victory'; or for Louis Pasteur, 'Science', 'discovery', etc. As I have mentioned, the master signifiers have shadowy negative counterparts in the unconscious, but in these Discourses, S1 is the flaunted version: it is *what is perceived to be the most important thing about the person* by others; for instance, in the Master's and in the University's Discourse.

S2 here represents 'knowledge' – in French, '*savoir*', which is pure knowledge with a connotation of 'ability', as opposed to '*connaissance*', which in English would suggest knowledge in the sense of familiarity (like knowing a person). $ is the subject barred by its submission to language and castration, and therefore conscious of its lack and in search of an object cause of desire; a is the object cause of desire (*l'objet petit a*) that, in the first Discourse, Lacan gives the status of 'surplus enjoyment', in the sense of what is produced by the worker. The arrows indicate the direction of action in the relationship between members of the algorithm. There is no direct relationship between $ and a, as the Subject has no direct access to the object of its desire.

The Discourse of the Master

This is the first Discourse, which provided the template for the others. In the Discourse of the Master, the agent/truth/other/production relationship is thus:

The master signifier (of the Master) is the agent of communication and instead of addressing the other, addresses 'the knowledge' in his/her place; in other words, the Master is addressing the other not as a Subject but in his/her functional role – because of his/her ability or knowledge (as a servant, soldier, artisan, etc.). An example would be a general in the army addressing precise orders to his troops: the general speaks not as a human being, but through his master signifiers – Rome/Britain/'the Motherland', etc. – *this* is what addresses the soldier, who is important only in his knowledge of how to fight. The truth of the master signifier – that the agent (the general in this case) is actually a barred Subject and as lacking as everyone else – is 'hidden'; however, beneath that master signifier, the barred Subject is enjoying the production of the knowledge of the soldiers – he is enjoying the fight they will put up for him.

Another example would be a company boss addressing a hireling – let us say an events organiser. He orders her to organise a party for him, but it is not the individual he is addressing, it is her expertise in events management. She receives the order not from the boss as a human Subject, but via his master signifiers as an important and rich employer, and produces the event, the success of which feeds back and is enjoyed by him in his castratedness, assuaging his anxiety.

The Discourse of the University

It is interesting that Lacan chose to speak of the Discourse of the University and not of the Academic (*universitaire*); it seems that he wished to make a point about the functioning of institutions, and by extension of the individuals within them in their capacity of incarnating the institution. He had great experience, after all, of the tendency of people to identify with their institutions, usually to no particularly creative end. The formulation for this is:

Knowledge – what the institution is supposed to embody – is at the place of the agent; it addresses the other – here, the *objet petit a* of a student. The truth, hidden beneath the embodiment of knowledge, is the master signifier of the institution (which may be 'important', 'historic', 'venerable'); and beneath the object cause of desire is hidden the barred subject, the castratedness of the student, who offers its productions to the knowledge but in fact is motivated by the master signifiers of the institution, which feed into his/her *objet petit a*. Knowledge occupies the place of the agent, which addresses itself to the object cause of desire, as the desire for knowledge is, after all, the supposed reason why the student is there. But in this relationship, one can see that the *objet petit a* is also, and perhaps as importantly, fed into by the master signifiers of the institution, and these contribute endlessly to the castratedness of the Subject of the student. Perhaps the student imagines that it can overcome the splitting of his/her Subject by absorbing these master signifiers. In addressing the knowledge not to the Subject, but to the object cause of desire of the Subject, what is 'produced' is, in fact, more castratedness: the castration of the student seems to be exacerbated by his/her position within the institution. Beneath the appearance of dispensing knowledge, the University controls the Subject by means of its master signifiers ('Sorbonne', 'honour', 'international prestige', etc.), and enjoys – as the Master enjoys the fruits of the labours of his Slave – the 'production' of the castrated student. The institution is also guilty of giving the impression to the student that by careful attention and absorption of its master signifiers, she/he may overcome his/her castration.

This is a system of functioning that is common to all institutions: one can see it at work in corporations, professions, and government departments – indeed in any institution where 'knowledge' in some form takes the place of the agent which addresses discourse, and acts as a lure to the other's desire. The world is full of individuals who have worked or studied within institutions and come to realise that they learn more outside, and that the main interest of the institution is in perpetuating its fantasy of itself – in maintaining, brightly polished, its master signifiers. It is equally full of people who have adopted the master signifiers of their institutions as their own, in a position of hysterical identification, imagining that in belonging to a 'venerable' or 'dynamic' or 'powerful' institution, they too acquire these characteristics. Others again have been made to feel more and more helpless, small, and castrated by the institution over the years.

The Discourse of the Analyst

The formulation here is:

$$\uparrow \frac{a}{S2} \begin{matrix} \longrightarrow \\ \times \end{matrix} \frac{\$}{S1} \downarrow$$

In this, you can see that the Analyst has accepted becoming, symbolically, the *objet petit a* of the analysand. This is one of the most usual roles the analyst has to accept; he/she is, after all, an empty mirror upon which everything may be reflected, and when in full transference, the analysand will be addressing his/her object cause of desire. So now, in this case, in his/her role as the *objet petit a*, the Analyst addresses his/her discourse to the castratedness, the anxiety, of the patient, and his/her questioning pushes the analysand to produce a master signifier which is reflected back to the Analyst, while the hidden knowledge of the Analyst, in the place of truth, is fed into the castrated Subject, fuelling the production by it of master signifiers. The Analyst is the 'Subject-supposed-to-know', and the knowledge (about the analysand) is 'hidden' beneath the Analyst, who appears as the object cause of desire; but the analysand will discover that the knowledge of its own desire is not held by the Analyst but revealed through its master signifier. The Analyst does not adopt a position of power like the Master, or of knowledge, like the University, and because of that, is often considered subversive by institutions.

The Discourse of the Hysteric

It must first be pointed out that one doesn't have to be hysterical in the clinical sense to hold the Discourse of the Hysteric; indeed, Lacan made it clear that this type of discourse, in non-hysterical people, is precisely what leads to true learning. Here, the agent of the discourse is the castrated lackingness of the Hysteric; hidden beneath its bar is his/her object cause of desire. This barred Subject, driven by its *objet petit a*, addresses the master signifiers of the other, which respond with the production of knowledge, beneath the bar. It is to the master signifier that the Hysteric addresses his/her questions, but she/he receives as an answer only the knowledge of that person, which Hysteric enjoys for want of anything better, although these answers never constitute a satisfactory response to his/her desire. The Master's willingness to answer the questions of the Hysteric is not fuelled by his/her wish to teach but is an effect of the unconscious connection with the *objet petit a* of the Hysteric, as represented by the oblique arrow. The hysterical questioning pushes the master signifier up to the limits of its knowledge and leads to the Hysteric's frustration when this limit is reached. The Discourse of the Hysteric is held by anyone who is on the path to knowledge; indeed, Lacan says that the desire for knowledge does not lead to knowledge, and what *does* is precisely the Discourse of the Hysteric.

In the Discourse of the University, one can see that the barred subject of the student in fact responds indirectly to the master signifier of the institution, as much as to the knowledge. The primary relationship of the student is with what is represented by the institution, and not with knowledge; the student wants to have the *status of one who knows*, rather than the knowledge itself. Curiously, the position of the Hysteric, which is incessantly to question the Master, results in the acquisition of knowledge. While she/he truly wants to know what is his/her object cause of desire, she/he gets fed knowledge instead, and without setting out to become one who knows, ends up knowing.

This is very much the position adopted by good journalists, when they are in the field. It is a position that requires (as shown in the barred Subject as the addressing agent) perfect acceptance of one's ignorance, no great desire to pretend to any other status, and a hunger for the object cause of desire. It is a position in which the Subject can question the other – who is represented by master signifiers – with an unquestioning acceptance of the authority of those master signifiers: *this man before me is an Afghan warlord, I expect him to know about his territories … this woman is a botanist, therefore I must ask her about plants …*

Oddly enough, apart from hysterics and journalists, there are not many people who pose questions to others precisely and exhaustively in their true field of expertise: we do not necessarily respond to the master signifiers of the other, because of other social and unconscious factors. Indeed, many social relationships require one to ignore the master signifiers of the other: for instance, if you meet a famous writer at a party, you may feel that interrogating her about her work might be tiresome to her; if you consult an expert for an opinion (say, on a legal matter), it is a commercial transaction in which you would be overstepping the boundaries by questioning him about the workings of his field more generally. The student is *in theory* permitted to question his/her teachers/superiors in such a way, but in fact rarely does. This may be because the castratedness she/he feels in relation to the institution is such that she/he feels 'stupid' or embarrassed about asking, or she/he can't be bothered because what she/he hankers after is the qualification or status the institution will give him/her rather than the knowledge itself, or if she/he does pose questions these may be designed to 'show off' in some bid to identify with the master signifiers of the institution. It is only those who take up the Hysteric's discourse – who put their castratedness on the line, as it were, who truly gain knowledge. The journalist's role on the other hand *requires* him/her to adopt the Hysteric's discourse for long periods of their career, and the result of this may be that they end up with an encyclopaedic knowledge of a great many things.

11

Can one train an analyst?

It was because of Lacan's personality and practice – in particular the duration of his sessions – that he was denied recognition as a training analyst by the International Psychoanalytic Association (IPA), and rejected by any French group that wanted IPA recognition. There was a whiff of the Holy Inquisition in the manner in which the IPA conducted its 'fact-findings' about Lacan's practices – the picking off of individuals for interrogations in closed sessions, the Hobson's choice presented to his trainees – *renounce Lacan or be struck off yourself* ... And as in the Inquisition, the *substance* of the heresy was never discussed – only '*Has it been committed?*' The Church, at least in its early days, did enter into debate upon theological grounds, as at the Council of Nicaea, which established Arianism as a heresy, but the Turquet Commission – and the one before it chaired by Winnicott – never wanted to know the theoretical basis for the use of variable duration sessions, or for any other aspect of Lacanian practice.

The animosity that Lacan arouses even today is extraordinary. It is possible to find on the Internet articles vilifying Lacan, written by people too young ever to have met the man, or by people who haven't read his work; and always, these critics attack the man and not his theories – unless it's to say they are incomprehensible. In France, passions run perhaps even higher: we have heard psychologists almost beside themselves with aggression against ... *what*? It is hard to know what it is he represents to them, but it is certain that his Subject is still the object of strong projections. And any analyst who admits to being Lacanian is open too to the same strange projections, which are perhaps the legacy of the IPA's inquiry. Just as the Holy Inquisition made the signifier 'heretic' equate almost with the devil, the Turquet Commission made 'Lacan' equal 'perverse and dangerous'.

The IPA did not, of course, set out consciously to achieve this effect, but there is something in the *process* of inquisition that generates angels and demons, and crushes rational thought. It perverts the development of a field of study by disallowing discussion around the real issue – which is the practice and training of analysts – and it terrorises the community into not being able to think clearly about these things. How it does this is by determining the 'sin' *in advance* of the process, so all that's left for the Commission to discover is whether or not it has been committed. The 'punishment' is, of course, the threat of excommunication – which for practising analysts, means their careers and sometimes their livelihoods. This is an abuse of power that is anti-intellectual, but perhaps it hits hardest the people who wield it, for *they* cannot think about the ideas at stake; it hits at those who are interrogated, for it requires them to renounce their trainer and therefore their own intellectual heritage; and hits the psychoanalytical community as a whole, which has never been able to have a theoretical discussion about practice and training – except within the tight confines of what had already been decided by its first popes.

There is an apocryphal story that Galileo, after recanting everything he had discovered about the earth moving around the sun at his inquisition, was heard to mutter as he left the court: 'And yet, it moves!' One wonders what Lacan's trainees – men who had been on his couch several times a week for months or years – might have muttered to themselves after their interrogation by the Turquet Commission; certainly, they said nothing for years afterwards. The leading figures of the French psychoanalytical establishment – Jean Laplanche, Jean-Bertrand Pontalis, Didier Anzieu, and Daniel Widlöcher – were all Lacan's trainees who had renounced him. However, they had been trained, and indelibly marked, by him, and were too old to begin another training to 'erase' his contamination. Those whose own theories came to look curiously like Lacan's never cited him or his influence; one or two, towards the end of their careers, admitted in interviews that 'he had not really been so bad'. The French psychoanalytic establishment after the Turquet Commission became a strange community – a double-image of post-occupation France, where there were vast areas of '*non-dit*' – subjects that could not be mentioned.

On the other side, the persecution of Lacan turned his followers into disciples: they defended him to the hilt, because in doing so, they were defending themselves; but this defensive position led to a lack of critical discourse and perhaps to the self-indulgences Lacan became noted for at the end of his life. Those disciples who have admitted that for the last five years or so of his life the Master had begun to behave oddly, have done so under their breath. If he did not know when to quit, or when he was becoming unreasonable, it was perhaps because there was no one who would tell him. A tendency towards uncritical reverence for the Master *did* develop in some Lacanian circles; fortunately – and this is not intended facetiously – the difficulty in understanding exactly what Lacan meant makes it quite hard for anyone to claim to be the one true interpreter of his words. Also, Lacan himself, perhaps because of his great distrust of institutions in themselves, was as iconoclastic towards his own works – creating and destroying schools and systems, altering his own formulations and encrypting them in mathemes, so that the Lacanian community remains itself fragmented, lacking in any one 'vatican' body.

What makes an analyst?

It was on training issues that the IPA excommunicated Lacan, and it should be remembered that the issue of the training and accreditation of analysts was a source of controversy from the very start of the psychoanalytical movement. From the 1920s, there was tension between the Americans and Europeans over it, with the Americans insisting upon a system of accreditation that required a medical training as well; they felt that in their country, widespread 'quackery' made this necessary. However, it was perhaps also necessary for them to present psychoanalysis as 'scientific' because the dominant model for thinking about thinking across the Atlantic was Behaviourism, which depended on animals in laboratories, 'controlled' experiments, and various other trappings of science. In Europe, where psychoanalysis had evolved within hospital wards and was being enriched by intellectual currents from without, such a controlled system of accreditation and training seemed unnecessary; in addition, psychoanalysis was developing simultaneously along many different tracks, and it was impossible to find much agreement over the most basic theoretical questions. With no theoretical consensus, how would be it possible to formalise training or practical method?

The psychoanalysis of Sigmund Freud evolved by intuition coupled with medical clinical observation. It developed like a true natural science – by means of logical deduction and the postulation of models and hypotheses – and the only possible ways of assessing the correctness of these models is by a combination of pure logic and clinical observation. But it was an age when simple scientific certitudes had a great grip on the popular imagination, and the Americans fretted about accreditation and about regulating practice. The battle to control psychoanalysis was already well under way at the outbreak of World War II, which easily tipped the balance of power over to the Americans.

European voices were scattered and silenced, the British represented Europe, and although they put up a struggle, they were forced to accept the American way. When the French psychoanalytical world emerged from the shadows of occupation, they found that the landscape had changed: IPA accreditation was now necessary for an analyst to be recognised as such in the wider world, and the Société Psychanalytique de Paris (SPP – the only French psychoanalytical organisation of the time) had to come up with a system of training and accreditation that fitted with the rules of the now American-controlled IPA.

Given the history of controversy over training, it is not surprising that the first schism in French psychoanalysis happened over this issue. In the refashioning of the SPP after the war, it was decided that training should be regulated by an institute, and should follow strict and medical rules. The statutes laid down were judged unacceptable by many SPP members, and a group of 'modern' analysts led by Daniel Lagache, Françoise Dolto, and Juliette Favez-Boutonnier left the SPP in 1953. Lacan, who had recently been appointed President of the SPP and director of the new training institute, sympathised with their position and joined them; with him, around half of his pupils who were training analysts of the SPP also left. Their new group was called the Société Française de Psychanalyse (SFP).

The nub of the problem was what *is* an analyst? The classical institutional answer is that an analyst is a member of an analytical group/institution: it is *membership* that makes a real analyst. A process of obtaining membership is supposed to guarantee 'quality'; but does it? The SPP's process was, briefly, this: as well as some theoretical learning, you have to go through an analysis yourself, and then take on a couple of patients in supervised analysis – where you alternate sessions with the analysand with sessions with your trainer, talking to him/her about the process – and then, after these supervised analyses are over, you may get your accreditation. For Lacan and the other the SFP members, this was not good enough. Lacan held that an analyst is someone who is competent in allowing an analytical process to take place between the analysand and themselves without letting their own symptoms get in the way of the analysand's work – and it is perfectly imaginable that someone could go through all the hoops and still, at the end of a 'perfect cursus' of training, be a rather neurotic individual unable safely to occupy the place of the analyst in the treatment. In particular, he was conscious of the danger of the idea of 'didactic analysis' on offer from the SPP; he and other SFP members felt that requiring someone to undergo analysis *in order to become* an analyst contaminates the personal analytical work and actually strengthens the neuroses that were in place before.

Many people would think that some analysis, be it undertaken for professional or for personal reasons, is better than none at all. Lacan's view was that an analysis undertaken for professional reasons could be worse than none at all. This is because a successful analysis depends very much on the sincere engagement *and need* of the analysand, and if this person is able to justify their presence on the couch as a professional rather than a personal necessity, it is likely to fail.

The quarrel

It is a central tenet of Lacanian practice that the nature and outcome of the treatment is highly dependent upon the dynamics of the need, demand, and desire of the patient. If the patient is there for professional reasons, this changes the nature of the demand (and thereby the desire to be cured that arises in the gap between need and demand): the demand is no longer to be cured of emotional pain, and when this demand is not there, there can be no working through of neuroses. Furthermore, as anyone who has the experience of analysis knows, once you open your mouth, you cannot help but engage (to some extent) in the process; therefore, in the absence of a true demand to be helped, the Subject, in talking, develops more and more sophisticated methods of skirting around the core issues, building upon the neurotic structures of repression and ego already in place. Incomplete analysis hardens the neurosis: one may think one knows more about oneself (and indeed, may know a little more), but what isn't known is now embedded in an impenetrably armoured edifice. Such false 'work' is probably supported and encouraged by the notion of 'training analysis' – part of the SPP route to accreditation.

That was the basis of the quarrel between Lacan and the SPP. However, the politics of IPA accreditation was to hound him and his supporters far beyond this point. A further schism was to occur, this time within the group founded by Daniel Lagache, which Lacan had joined – the SFP. This group was comprised of people who shared Lacan's theoretical views about training, and the split was caused by pressure from the IPA for them to 'denounce' Lacan.

All the analysts of the SFP wanted to be members of the IPA – 'internationally recognised psychoanalysts'. But the IPA had Lacan marked out as trouble, because of his use of variable duration sessions and his generally maverick attitude. The wish of the IPA to get rid of Lacan put the members of the SFP in a dilemma. Whether or not they agreed with Lacan's views, they had to say they didn't in order to become members of the IPA. The only area in which the IPA could fault Lacan's practice was the duration of the sessions, and as they did not wish to discuss theory with him, they focused on his personality and said that he was dangerous – 'seductive' – as a trainer. Some SFP members could not sacrifice their careers out of loyalty to Lacan: they left and created their own group, the Association Psychanalytique de France (APF), and as they had 'renounced' Lacan under interrogation by the Turquet Commission, they were given IPA recognition.

Exclusion and new beginnings

Lacan was again out in the cold, and now branded as 'unfit' as a training analyst, while the people he had trained rose to the highest positions in the psychoanalytic establishment. Undeterred by the IPA ruling, Lacan (with the supporters who remained loyal to him) founded his own school, the Ecole Française de Psychanalyse, soon to be rebaptised Ecole Freudienne de Paris. In his founding text about its work in 1964, Lacan created the principle of the 'cartel' – a small group of three to five training analysts, or analysts working on theoretical questions with an additional one who chairs the work. These cartels were designed to allow intense theoretical work – the idea being that an individual working alone might become lazy or complacent in his/her productions. The cartels were to last only a couple of years and to change in composition to avoid the negative effects of habit and over-familiarity. Still faced with the difficult issue of training, Lacan in 1967 proposed a new process – '*la passe*'. This process became properly institutionalised in 1969 but led to the departure of some senior analysts of the EFP, Pierra Aulagnier and François Perrier, who left the school to create their own organisation, the OPLF (Organisation Psychanalytique de Langue Française).

The '*passe*' was created by Lacan as a way of accessing the title of *Analyste de l'Ecole*, which had been reserved up until 1967 for the initial members who created the school. The candidate to the '*passe*' – called the *passant* – was supposed to bear witness of his/her experience of analysis – talking about it to two other people, the *passeurs*. The role of the *passeurs* was to transmit the content of that testimony to an 'agreement jury'. The jury's president was Lacan and the other members were analysts with the title of *Analyste de l'Ecole*, elected by the general assembly of the school. The *passe* was in some ways the end of the analysand's analysis – when she/he dropped his/her analyst as

Subject-supposed-to-know; the transference of the analysand is radically changed in this process, and his/her analyst becomes no longer an omnipotent figure but just a 'remainder'.

Ironically, it is not impossible that Lacan, when creating the *passe*, had in mind the effects of the Turquet Commission on some of his own analysands. He had seen how some of them moved away from him following their interviews with the Commission – as if talking about him was the act which toppled the analyst from his pedestal. It is an indication of Lacan's spirit that he could see in a situation intended to be a blow to him the seeds of an idea he could use in his work: that such an interview could be used to mark the proper end of the analysis, as a 'closure'.

It was at this time that Lacan mentioned that 'the psycho-analyst derives his authority only from himself'.[1] This statement, which led to an outcry amongst IPA members, did not mean that anybody could be an analyst, but was in fact a criticism of the IPA regulation that allowed the accreditation of analysts provided they go through a certain period of being analysed and then of 'didactic' analysis. For Lacan, this was not rigorous enough: his statement was meant to point out that only *some* of the people who go through this process might truly make that psychological shift from the position of the analysand into the position of the analyst. His statement also highlighted the diffi-cult-to-define nature of what makes a good analyst – and it is still the case that titles and certificates are no guarantees of effec-tiveness, while the insightful interventions of a 'lay' person may have an immensely therapeutic effect. It also meant, more pragmatically, that only the individual is the guarantor of his/her ethics and honesty: once the door of the office is shut, only the analyst knows the reality of his/her practices, the limitations of his/her talent, and the extent to which his/her own neurosis can interfere with the analytical process. These are all things that no commission, committee, or exam board can control or guarantee. At this stage in his career, Lacan's statement was not a provocation aimed at shocking the establishment, but probably a real reflection about the loneliness and high responsibility of the individual who dares to occupy the place of the analyst, and of the need to continue to think about and refine the methods and criteria for accreditation.

After Lacan

La passe was considered a failure very early on, even before Lacan's death, but the Ecole de la Cause Freudienne (ECF), directed by Lacan's son-in-law, has continued using it. But perhaps in memory of the anti-institutional, anti-regulatory spirit of Lacan, training issues have remained a cause of continual self-questioning for the ECF. Some of the school's documents about training question the training effect of an analysis: 'the training effect of analytical treatment is distinguishable from its therapeutic effect. It is not possible to predict the training effect of an analysis. It can only be judged by its results at the end – the conclusion of the treatment.' The use of the *passe* is precisely to assess the training effect of one's analysis. Having put the training effect of the analysis at the heart of the training of the analysis, the ECF nonetheless asks:

> These subjective mutations which happened during the treatment of the subject – the analytical treatment of the subject and the knowledge that the subject has acquired – are they enough to guarantee its training, or is it necessary to acquire a knowledge external to the experience – the analytical experience itself: the one of clinical practice, of reading analytical texts and texts of sciences that bring something to psychoanalysis?

So the ECF teaches, but remains ambivalent towards its teaching: 'Teaching is not just a programme but works also because of the immersion of the subject in the work of the school and of the time actively spent at this work. This training is not only clinical, but also ethical and political. This training questions the relationship of the subject to the analytical discourse.' The ECF does not deny the need for some kind of external knowledge on top of analytical experience but insists that it is quite important to think about the relationship between these two types of knowledge in a very particular way. 'These forms of knowledge have to be explored again and subverted by the point of non-knowledge reached during the personal analysis'.[2]

In a strangely parallel way, the APF, founded by the group of analysts who left Lacan during the second schism and returned to the lap of the IPA, still insist upon their difference, claiming to be the 'French exception' within the IPA. They describe the way the APF trains its analysts with the word 'extraterritoriality' (normally a legalistic term to denote the status of a foreign embassy, which is exempt from the laws of the country in which it stands). The training committee may admit or refuse a candidate to the institute of training, without the candidate being told before on which criteria the selection will be done: only his/her own analytical experience can guide him/her. The APF full members are all full members of the IPA and are automatically training analysts for the APF training institute. Analysts in training remain trainees until their training is fully validated and they become full members. The APF has got rid of didactic analysis, thinking that the institution should not be involved in the personal analysis of the candidate. They admit candidates whose analysis has been with an analyst of another analytical society, including a Lacanian one, and even if someone has been analysed by an analyst in training; the APF prides itself on its openness in examining the request of someone coming from an 'unknown couch'.

However, the training at the APF is rather more structured than all this may suggest: the procedure, even if apparently very open, is extremely long, and presents many hoops through which the candidate must jump. First of all, the candidate must have been or must still be in an analysis when she/he contacts the training committee for a possible admission to the training institute. It is also desirable but not compulsory that the candidate is a medical doctor or a psychologist. The committee is composed of nine analysts with a third of it new each year, and as a first step, the candidate is sent a list of the nine members out of which she/he must choose three with whom to have an initial interview. These three analysts then report to the committee about the interview, recommending whether or not to take the candidature further. If the candidate gets over this hurdle, she/he is allowed to follow the teaching of the institute, to participate in their scientific and academic meetings, and will also undertake a first 'controlled' or monitored treatment. This involves having an adult analysand on the couch three times a week, and simultaneously undertaking two weekly sessions with the training analyst (although the institute doesn't use this term, and calls the person the 'controller'). Following this first supervised treatment, a second is introduced, and these two successive supervised treatments must last at least ten years. The final assessment of the training is decided by a college of full members after they have received a report written by one of them. The author of the report has had a long interview with the candidate, and all the candidate's training and personal analysis is discussed: seminars, scientific activities, hospital or university career, analytical practice, articles, books, etc. ... Acceptance to the title of *analyste titulaire* is made by the college of members on the proposal of the rapporteur, unless the rapporteur or a member requests a discussion and vote. In this way, the training process of the AFP is more rigorous than that of the SPP.

The SPP's main area of rigour lies in 'club membership': candidates must be in analysis with one of their own members, and preferably one of their accredited training analysts. A candidate who has been in analysis with someone outside – for instance, if she/he comes from another country – must recommence an analysis with an SPP member, even if they've already been 'on the couch' for ten years. The SPP's practices have remained faithful to the IPA standards in matters of training. The personal analysis has to take place at least three times a week for sessions that last at least 45 minutes. The candidate will have at least two cases of analysis in supervision and the supervision lasts between two and five years.

12
Lacanian practice

The status of the unconscious, which, as I have shown, is so
fragile on the ontic plane, is ethical. In his thirst for truth, Freud
says, *Whatever it is, I must go there*, because somewhere, this
unconscious reveals itself.

(Lacan, *The Four Fundamental Concepts of Psychoanalysis*)

The myths of silence, brevity, and callousness

It is rumoured that Lacanian analysts never say a thing, and that
the ten-minute sessions are mostly filled by silence; furthermore,
it is said that Lacanians are not really interested in curing their
patients. It is also rumoured that Lacan even had his hair cut
during a session – a story put about to suggest that he held his
patients in dreadful contempt. Inquisitions have such a demonis-
ing effect; two centuries earlier, baby-killing and well-poisoning
may also have been mentioned.

Lacan used sessions of variable duration, and the variability of
duration was an important tool for him; if he might terminate a
session after ten minutes, he might equally keep the next one
going for fifty. Years after the end of his analysis with Lacan,
Daniel Widlöcher revealed in an interview that it had involved
four sessions of around half an hour each every week.[1] Other
analysands at the same period described often having very short
sessions. It is likely that the 'personality' of each of these
analysands was quite different and Lacan used the short sessions
on purpose. However, very often when he used short sessions,

he would offer to see his analysands more frequently, sometimes almost every day.[2]

For Lacan, ending the session was *a meaningful act* and too important to leave to mere form; it was not good enough to end a session just because the allotted time was up, especially if the analysand was in the middle of some interesting discourse. Conversely, it may be useful to be able to end the session just at the point that the analysand says something important – so that it can 'hang in the air' for further reflection until the next time: more words will often obfuscate the realisation that was emerging. In many ways, the end of the session emphasises some particularly important aspect and works almost as an interpretation.

Also, the variability of duration itself is important in that if the analysand knows how long the session will last, she/he can use this as a 'way out', either spinning out unimportant stuff in order to avoid talking about something real, or – if they arrive at something important quite early on – then 'burying' it in empty talk until time is up, so that it is as good as forgotten. It is very common for analysands to 'play' a set duration to their own ends, hiding behind empty speech. Lacan saw it as important for the analyst to be able to end such a futile session as a way of signalling that she/he knows what the analysand is playing at, and that there's no point wasting both their time. This in itself forces analysands to be more honest: either they engage in some meaningful discourse or they drop out of analysis completely, but they can't pretend *to themselves* to be doing the work.

With brief sessions, Lacan aimed to 'stimulate' the analysand, but in order properly to use variable duration sessions, the analyst must be clear about the rationale behind them. They are difficult to handle without a minimum of talent and require full concentration on the part of the analyst and flawless honesty. They can be a precious and subtle instrument or simply hurtful. In Lacan's typically provocative words, 'With our short sessions, we managed to make a male subject talk about his fantasy of anal pregnancy ... in a time frame where otherwise we would have been still discussing the art of Dostoyevsky.'[3]

What Lacanian analysis does not do

Before we go any further into what Lacanian analysis aims to do and how it tries to accomplish this, it is important to state first of all what it is *not*, and what its practitioners will not do. This is necessary because of the enormous range of different psychotherapeutic practices and theories available that offer precisely the things that Lacanian analysis would work *against*, or that use aspects of analysis in very different ways.

Lacanian practice does not make use of the phenomena of transference and counter-transference in the same way as other schools of psychoanalysis would. A Lacanian analyst does not enter into dialogue, except as a completely opaque mirror; a Lacanian analyst would not be 'sympathetic' or tell the patient how she/he (the analyst) feels. On the other hand, neither will a Lacanian analyst ever tell patients what are the roots of their feelings. A Lacanian will not point out to you that you are treating him/her like your mother/sister/lover, etc. or that your emotional reactions have been laid down according to this or that template, or at this or that moment of your childhood. Lacanian analysts use interpretations far, far more sparingly than do classical analysts, and almost never (or only in very particular circumstances) by direct reference to a theoretical construct.

A patient looking to boost his/her self-esteem, or to be reassured that she/he is really all right and just needs to rethink some of his/her 'coping strategies' should not go to a Lacanian analyst. Lacanian analysis does not 'strengthen' or 'support' the ego; all the manifestations of 'ego' that are considered today to be innate human rights – self-esteem, sense of identity, self-image, etc. – are precisely what Lacanian analysis dismantles, bolt by bolt, nut by nut, in order to allow the patient to come face to face with his/her own Subject, and at last to recognise it, on his/her own terms.

Lacanian analysis does not set out as its goal the curing of symptoms. Unlike many therapies on offer, which promise to cure this or that problem within six sessions or ten or twelve, Lacanian analysis would never make such a claim. One has only to cast one's mind back to his theory of the *sinthome* to see that to Lacan, symptoms occupied too important and central a place in the Subject's Borromean knot to be so carelessly cut out, according to some easy-to-follow pattern, in six sessions. If symptoms disappear during the course of analysis, then that is 'extra'; this position arises from Lacan's belief that patients have free will, and may choose to be cured or not to be cured, depending of the importance of the symptom in their personality structure. What is important is for them to have that free and conscious choice.

The mechanics of Lacanian practice

In outlining Lacanian technique, there is a point in beginning at the end – at the question *what is the point?* – for the objective of an exercise justifies its practices. So, what is the point of Lacanian analysis? We cannot categorically deny the charge that Lacanians don't really try to cure their patients; there is a grain of truth in this, although it depends upon what you define as 'curing'. We have already seen the trepidation with which Lacan approached the removal of symptoms, and perhaps the only justification for doing it at all is the demand of the patient to be cured, perhaps without any full understanding of what this entails.

The Lacanian analyst who undertakes to guide the patient upon this risky journey knows that at some point during the course of the analysis, the patient will be faced again with a decision – to be cured of his/her symptom, or not to be – but the difference between this decision and the same one taken at the start of the journey is that it should now be an enlightened choice, made in the light of self-knowledge. Furthermore, as the symptom is part of the Subject's structure, the treatment can't fully eradicate it, but always leaves a residue – the foundations of the symptom – the *sinthome*. If the patient chooses to give up the symptom, there may be the problem of the space it used to fill, which may generate the need for a continuation of analysis.

As an example: *a gay man has been in analysis for some years. His problem is that he isn't happy being gay; after many years, he has come to admit to himself that what he wants is to have children, to be a father. He disapproves of gay adoptions and thinks he could only be truly happy with a woman; yet he continues to have casual sex with men. He has come to understand the source of his neuroses; he has traced them accurately back to childhood, and enunciated with full recognition some of his master signifiers.* As far as the analyst is concerned, this could be the end of the analysis: the choice now (whether to become 'straight' or to stay gay) is for the patient to make freely. If he chooses to 'go straight', then a whole new set of issues will arise, and these may or may not be the subject of a different treatment.

Unlike Klein or Anna Freud or practitioners of American Ego Psychology, Lacan would never have set out the goals of analysis, because the goal for each and every patient would be different, and it would anyway almost certainly shift during the analysis. Melanie Klein once claimed that the outcome of analysis was that 'repressions lessen while the ego gains in strength and coherence; the cleavage between idealised and persecutory objects diminishes; the phantastic aspects of objects lose in strength; all of which implies that unconscious phantasy life – less sharply divided off from the unconscious part of the mind – can be better utilised in ego activities.'[4] One wonders how she could state with such certainty the desirability of some of these effects, given how little agreement existed about the concepts mentioned: the ego, the unconscious, the role and functioning of phantasy (unconscious fantasies), etc.

There has been a tendency in some areas of psychoanalysis and psychology to deal with things by giving them new labels, which allows a re-arranging of the drawers in which they can be filed away, thereby giving the impression that something has been deeply considered and understood. Lacan never used a new label where an old one would do (for instance preferring to talk about 'aggressiveness in analysis' and 'resistance' as distinct phenomena rather than dumping them together in the fashionable drawer of 'negative transference') and, typically of his caution, he refused to spell out simple goals.

In the formulation of various of his theoretical precepts, he speaks about the need to 'accompany the subject towards … the point at which the objective "me" and the subjective "I" can be reunited'. This implies getting past the obscuring edifice of the ego, which is the fiction the Subject has constructed out of its desires and fears. He suggests that the revelation of the authentic desire of the Subject in its own words is one of the aims of analysis: 'The function of the signifier as such in desire's quest is … the key to what we need to know in order to terminate our analyses – and no artifice can make up for it if we are to achieve this end.'[5] But when talking about the aims of analysis directly, he becomes circumspect, preferring not to commit himself to any easy pronouncements. In his paper on 'The Direction of the Treatment and the Principles of its Power', he only noted at the end of many pages of wide-ranging musings about transference, interpretation, and technique:

> Thus we have reached the tricky crux of this power that is ever open to a blind direction. It is the power to do good – no power has any other end – and that is why power has no end. But something else is at stake here: truth, the only truth, the

truth about the effects of truth. Once Oedipus set off down this path, he had already given up power. Where, then, is the direction of the treatment headed? Perhaps we need but question its means to define it in its soundness. Let us note:

1 that speech possesses all the powers here, the specific powers of the treatment;
2 that, with the fundamental rule of psychoanalysis, the analyst is far from directing the subject towards full speech, or toward a coherent discourse – rather, the analyst leaves the subject free to have a go at it;
3 that this freedom is what the subject tolerates least easily;
4 that demand is exactly what is put to one side in analysis, it being ruled out that the analyst satisfy any of the subject's demands;
5 that since no obstacle is put in the way of the subject's acceptance of his desire, it is toward this acceptance that he is directed and even channelled;
6 that resistance to this owning can, in the final analysis, be related here to nothing but desire's incompatibility with speech.

These points will all become clearer once we have talked more fully about Lacanian technique and the theory behind it; for now, it is interesting to note that Lacan, so often castigated for arrogance, should display such intellectual humility in refusing to impose rules and limits (and remember that a goal is itself a limit) upon the human science of psychoanalysis. Perhaps he wished to underline the fact that it was and is a developing field, and that over-prescriptiveness or making bold statements when in fact you are not completely sure, obscures the path for development.

None of this is to say that a patient should *not* go to a Lacanian analyst if she/he has a simple goal, for example, a symptom she/he wishes to be cured of; but if that patient chooses Lacanian analysis rather than one of those therapies that promises to cure you in ten sessions, then it follows that the patient *has already accepted* that the symptom is but a creation of his/her deep personality structure and is willing to try to discover that. The mother of a teenager with an eating disorder who was offered the choice between a quick-fix therapy and analysis with a Lacanian in the end chose the analyst, saying in explanation of her choice: '*It sounds like we could either cope with the problem or deal with it; I think it would be better to deal with it*'; she had understood, without being told, the difference between trying to pare off the visible manifestation of the problem or tackling its roots so that it won't grow back.

Likewise, the patient's goal may be to get out of a repetitious pattern of behaviour that causes him/her emotional pain; but again, in coming to a Lacanian analyst, the patient must be willing to assume all responsibility for his/her actions and feelings, for the analysis, if well done, will inevitably lead to the patient's encounter with the bare truth of his/her Subject, hidden for all his/her life behind his/her ego.

It is not possible to describe or explain the mechanics of a Lacanian analysis without recourse to theory, and without wishing to repeat what has already been said elsewhere in this book, I would remark that three concepts that are important here are that of the Other, that of the formation of the Subject in the Mirror Stage, and that of desire – its objects and its structuring force.

Some points to bear in mind are:

- The ego is the lie the patient tells him/herself. It is a fictional creation of the Subject founded upon the love of its image, and the discourse of the Other. It is in the maintenance of this fiction that a signifying chain must be repressed into the unconscious. The analytical process should not aim at 'strengthening' the ego but quite the reverse: 'The imaginary of the ego must give way … to the subject in the authenticity of his desire'[6] (and this is where we begin to get woven into Lacan's intricate web of interplay of desire, need, and demand in analysis, but for the moment, we must hold this off as a distraction).

- The knowledge the patient seeks is already known to him/her: it exists in his/her unconscious, in the signifying chain containing the master signifiers. This is the 'knowledge' that slips out in dreams, slips of the tongue, self-defeating acts – and, of course, the symptoms that might have prompted the Subject to come to the couch in the first place. Analysis seeks to trace the signifying chain, bringing out of the unconscious more and more of its links.

- The truth can only be arrived at by means of the master signifiers, the 'negative side' of which must be drawn out of the unconscious. The *true* signifying chain – not the one spun by the 'de-negatives' of the master signifiers – has to be built of the Subject's own volition; 'telling' it to him/her will only lead to a fresh repression of it, or of enough elements of it as will render it meaningless. At best, the analyst may 'supply' at the right moment, a missing element, but the job of inserting it into the chain is the patient's sole and sovereign right.

- The Other – the set of rules and hypotheses into which the individual is born and which includes and is contained within language – creates the Subject and its ego; as language, it is the raw material from which the signifying chain was produced; its first embodiment – the mother – is the object of primary identification of the child.

- The first transference in psychoanalysis must mimic that of the primary identification, so that the analyst embodies the Other – the gatekeeper of the meanings of the signifiers used by the analysand.

- The analyst is the *'sujet suppose savoir'*: the Subject-supposed-to-know; the analysand makes the hypothesis that the analyst knows things about him/her that she/he (the Subject) doesn't. This hypothesis is important because in making it, the analysand recognises that *there is something to know* – something to which she/he is oblivious, which is the first truth in analysis. Analysis works by the readiness of this Subject-supposed-to-know to listen to the patient, and his/her ability to reflect back at the patient, with the accuracy of the 'pure mirror of a smooth surface' (i.e. without distortion), the knowledge contained in the patient's own signifiers.

- Desire is what sustains the analysis, and it is the analyst's job to sustain desire. Desire is also, together with its twin, anxiety, one of the principal structuring forces of the Subject; it is a condition in the Subject that the ego is often oblivious to, and one of the aims of analysis is to allow the Subject to bring its authentic desires into the light of consciousness.
- The role of the analyst is threefold: to be the 'pure mirror', to be the Other, and to sustain desire.

Transference in Lacanian analysis

Unlike Klein and Anna Freud, Lacan never recommended talking to the patient about his/her transference – what she/he was feeling towards the analyst, etc.; indeed, he warned against this practice, which he felt engaged the ego of the patient – the very part responsible for blocking out truth – to the further obscuring of the Subject. However, the constant and ever-changing manifestations of transference in an analysis had to be noted with great precision by the analyst, and 'played' with extreme subtlety by the analyst, who should be as opaque and reflective as possible – an empty mirror. 'Throughout the course of the analysis, on the sole condition that the ego of the analyst agrees not to be there, on the sole condition that the analyst is not a living mirror but an empty mirror, what happens, happens between the ego of the subject and the others.'[7] In other words, the analyst has to put to one side his/her ego, and listen impassively, like a 'pure mirror of absolute smoothness', so as to allow the patient to project upon him/her the successive images of the myriad interlocutors the patient has had in his/her life; the 'others' in this sentence refers to these interlocutors (often the mother, father, siblings, spouses). Lacan continues:

> The analysis consists in getting him to become conscious of his relations, not with the ego of the analyst, but with all those others who are his true interlocutors and whom he hasn't recognised. It is a matter of the subject gradually discovering which other he is truly addressing without knowing it, and of gradually assuming [coming to recognise and admit] the transferential relations at the place where he is, and where at first he didn't know he was.

Unlike classical analysts, Lacanian analysts tend not to point out to patients that they are talking to him/her as if he/she was their mother/ex-lover/grandfather, etc. unless he/she can do it subtly and in response to something the patients say; ideally, the patients should realise it themselves, as in the following example.

A woman had been addressing questions to her analyst for several sessions – they were all questions regarding her children – how she should behave towards them, how she should handle certain situations with them, etc. She seemed to be asking for practical advice, as one would of one's mother. The analyst said nothing much in response, until one day, the woman said: 'This is silly – I'm talking to you as if you were my mum!' To which the analyst replied, 'exactly so'.

In situations like these, a Lacanian analyst may also use the termination of the session as a form of interpretation: she/he may end the session there, to allow the analysand to understand that she/he has made a discovery of some significance, to reflect upon it further. In this manner, the variability of duration of the sessions is used as an interpretive tool.

Of course, it is not always possible for the patient to come to the realisation by themselves; in these cases, a Lacanian analyst could point it out. The difference with a classical analyst is that they would do it in such a way that their words came as a response to a question from the analysand, and the information would be couched in such a way as to focus purely on the fact of the transfer and not on the knowledge of the analyst implied in his/her act of pointing it out. For example, if a patient has been speaking for some time as if she/he thinks that the analyst holds certain opinions that the analyst knows were held by his/her father, the analyst may simply say: '*I'm not your father*' – thereby letting the patient see that she/he has been addressing her absent father, without allowing too much of an intrusion of the analyst's own being into the game at this point. A Lacanian would *not* say: '*Do you realise that for three sessions now you have been talking to me as if I were your father?*' because such a formulation would divert the patient's attention too much onto the ego of the analyst and the knowledge implied in her/his statement.

Lacan said that '*transference is the acting out of the reality of the unconscious*';[8] it arises not from the fact that the analyst reminds the analysand of somebody else, but because of the analysand's discourse and the unconscious knowledge it brings out.

As mentioned before, the most important identification that a Subject ever makes is the primary identification with the mother as Other. In analysis, there will be a re-enactment of this primary identification through transference: the analyst must assume the place that the mother occupied for the child with regard to the acquisition of language and the channelling of demand and need through the gateway of signifiers. This opens up the possibility of the patient hearing (reflected back by the mirror of the analyst) his/her signifiers in a new light. It happens at the start of the analysis, and not at the end, and by it the analyst is established in the place of the Other.

The primary identification allows for a series of transferences, by which the patient will identify the analyst as various different key figures in his/her past, and will behave towards the analyst accordingly. When this happens, 'the analyst must respond to them [the series of transferential discourses] only from his position in the transference'.[9] This is a point that will be taken up further when discussing the place of interpretation in Lacanian analysis.

Counter-transference and the question of the analyst's ego

Lacan describes counter-transference as 'the sum of the prejudices, passions, perplexities, and even the insufficient information of the analyst at a certain moment of the dialectical process of the treatment'. For Lacan, training analysis 'does not put the analyst beyond passion'.[10] But, if the analyst does not act on the basis of these feelings, it is not because his/her training analysis has drained away his/her passions, but because it has given him/her a desire which is even stronger than those passions: the desire of the analyst. 'No one has ever said that the analyst should never have feelings towards his patient. But he must know not only not to give into them, to keep them in their place, but also how to make adequate use of them in his technique.'[11]

The place of counter-transference in psychoanalysis is described by Lacan thus: 'The analyst's feelings have only one possible place in the game, that of the dummy ... if the dummy is revived the game will proceed without anyone knowing who is leading it.'[12] In other words, the analyst is aware of his/her feelings and takes them into account in his/her play, but doesn't play with them during the session; to do so would severely disturb the smooth surface of the mirror the analyst is supposed to be. If, for some reason, the analyst does decide to allow his/her feelings into play, then it must be done in such a way that the analysand remains unaware of it.

To return to the idea of the analyst as 'pure mirror', who has agreed to leave his/her ego at the door, it must be noted that when it came to the tricky business of making an interpretation, Lacan did not shy away from saying that this interpretation had necessarily to be made by the ego of the analyst. It is obvious, perhaps, that the analyst cannot 'cease to be' – the patient might as well be talking to a tape-recorder if that were the case. The place of the analyst's ego in making interpretations will be discussed in the section on interpretation.

Desire and demand in analysis

Transference helps the analysand to associate freely, and in analysis, the Subject will talk about all kinds of things it may normally avoid – these are usually its objects of desire, the containers within which the *agalma* of the small a object is located. (A distinction must be made at this point between the small a object and the container thereof – the object of desire, rather than the object *cause* of desire – as there is a tendency among Lacanian analysts to use '*l'objet petit a*' as a shorthand when in fact they are talking about its containers.) But here a problem often arises: these objects of desire are terribly fascinating to the Subject, who may remain stuck in their contemplation and be unable to produce any more meaningful discourse for quite some time. Many analyses founder completely on the rocks of the desired object; and as desire is itself desirable and a shield against anxiety, there is a natural resistance to doing anything that might endanger it.

A woman started an analysis after years of being involved in a series of painful relationships with married men; she can talk freely about the men in question, but cannot go further towards the small a object that she imagines to be in these men or to be attainable through the situation of the triangular relationship. She can describe the painful situations she was in and how she felt about them, but any discourse that begins to threaten her desire is quickly steered away from; it seems that the pain involved in those relationships is somehow preferable to the possible extinction of her desire. Without a skilful analyst, her analysis may have (and did for a while) become stalled at a point which many people reach just in talking to their friends (how often are friends called upon to listen sympathetically to the same problematic being described ad nauseam, often over the course of decades?). The analyst's job then is to oppose his/her desire to that of the analysand: and the analyst's desire can only be to cure the patient by helping him/her towards his/her own truth.

For Lacan, this desire of the analyst is even more important than transference phenomena, for this is the motor force that will keep the analysis going and prevent it becoming stalled: 'there is not only what the analyst intends to do with his patient, there is also what the analyst intends that his patient is going to make of himself'.[13]

Think how enormous is the task of the analyst – it is like breaching a city wall with a herring; analysis threatens the wall of ego around the Subject and undermines its foundation of desire ... so who could blame the Subject for resisting? And yet the analyst is supported by one thing – a traitor, if you like, inside the city wall – and that is the simple fact of the analysand having come to the session, which is the only indicator that she/he has *a desire to be cured*. This desire to be cured – at times apparently too feeble to do anything against the monument of ego constructed around the small a object – shows itself in the demands the patient puts upon the analyst. The analyst must play upon these demands to sustain that weak flame of desire-to-be-cured. And the analyst has some knowledge – not the knowledge she/he is supposed by the analysand to have, but the knowledge that '*desire is the desire of the Other*', and in his/her place as the Other, conferred by transference, she/he must play carefully with his/her weapons of silence and interpretation.

It is in order to sustain the primary demand – that of being cured – that the Lacanian analyst remains silent in response to the questions put to him/her by the patient. Those questions are a diversion from the real issue, and the patient probably knows that. What is important is that the patient is there and is still making demands; and by frustrating these demands, desire may be sustained:

> I keep quiet. Everybody agrees that by doing so I frustrate the speaker, and he knows that and I know it too. Why? If I frustrate him it is because he asks me for something – to answer him precisely – but he knows very well that it would be mere words, and he can get those from whomever he likes! It's not even certain that he'd be grateful to me if they were the right words, let alone if they were the wrong ones. It's not these words he is asking for. He is simply asking me … from the very fact he is speaking: his demand is intransitive … Of course his demand is deployed in the field of an implicit demand, that for which he is there: the demand to cure him, to reveal him to himself.[14]

And the frustration itself has a function other than that of sustaining desire: it is what may eventually cause the analysand to answer his/her own questions, from the unconscious knowledge she/he already has; in Lacan's words, it 'makes reappear the signifiers in which the frustration is held'.[15]

The Lacanian silence has another role; it is not only a frustrating silence, it is a silence in which the Subject's speech is 'borne aloft' – in the sense that a flag-bearer bears a flag.

> The analyst distinguishes himself in that he makes use of a function that is common to all people in a way that it not possible for everyone, when he bears the speech (like a flag-bearer). This is what he does with the Subject's speech, even when only welcoming it ... in the silence of the listener. This silence includes speech, as in the expression 'keeping silent' which with regard to the silence of the analyst does not only mean that he makes no noise, but that he keeps quiet rather than answers.[16]

It is only in the silence and in the presence of the Other embodied by the analyst that the Subject will ever be able to hear the resonance of its speech. This is why Lacan insists that there are questions to which his role is precisely *not to answer* – answers are, after all, available for free from sympathetic friends and always ignored ('*Do you think I should leave him?*' is an example; there is no answer to this that the analyst can possibly give; repeating it back is worse than meaningless, for it allows the Subject to hear it coming back to her from another person – disguising the fact that the question is *hers and hers alone*; silence would at least make *that* much clear).

For Lacan, as the analysis nears its end, the power of the analyst wanes, and finally, the analyst is discarded, like an empty shell. This contrasts strongly with the view of other schools of analysis that the end of an analysis should be closely controlled and managed by the analyst. In Lacanian analysis, the end is simply the point at which the patient's desire to be cured is no longer sufficiently strong to induce him/her to make the journey. The lessening of this desire should be the natural conse-quence of 'getting better', and the only thing that would inter-fere with it would be some badly handled transference in which a secondary desire has been created which supplants the primary one of being cured.

A final word on desire would be fitting here, but this time on the desire of the patient around which his/her ego is structured and which it is the task of analysis to discover. It is to remind the reader that desire is the foundation of the Subject's defences against anxiety, and the object cause of desire (a) has its inverse in the lack that causes anxiety, as shown in the formula

Unconscious   Spoken

$$\frac{S2}{\$} \quad \leftarrow\rightarrow \quad \frac{S1}{a}$$

(S1 being the spoken master signifier and S2 being its repressed counterfoil). Upon the foundation of desire and from the building blocks of language is constructed the ego of the Subject. From the blind gropings of the analysand's discourse will emerge the elements of the signifying chain that will enunciate his/her true desire, and maybe by extension, his/her castratedness.

But the construction of the chain is no easy matter; even when most of the elements have been brought to light, it remains for the analysand to put them together in the way that will reveal the right meaning (and remember, from linguistics, that it is the association of signifiers that gives meaning and not some 'natural' link between signifiers and signifieds). The point about the master signifiers is that they have a repressed counterpart which gives them meaning – the apparent signifieds of the master signifiers are unimportant. So let us now revisit our examples of chapters 8 and 3. The signifier 'sailing' for the man whose father was a keen sailor has importance only in its association with the father and with the situation of sibling rivalry in the home; without this, a boat is a boat and nothing else. Likewise, for the little girl, 'the best' is given weight and importance *because* of its counter-position with 'second best' and the chain of associations linked with this.

For Lacan, in order for the master signifiers to reveal their real meaning for the Subject, they have first to be 'dialectised' within the Subject's own mind – the analysand has to recognise the relationship between 'the best' and 'second best'; only then can the master signifier lose its tension – the tension of being coupled with its anxiogenic counterpart – and become uncoupled, a process Lacan called 'separation'.

This separation is the end of analysis: the point at which the little girl can truly feel that 'the best' has lost its importance, because it is no longer coupled with 'second best'. She may not stop wanting 'the best' of everything, but at least she may know why this is and be able to recognise when it is a nonsense (literally – that it has no sense outside the dialectic of her desire-anxiety, and thus has lost its tension); for only then can the alternative to 'the best' stop being so threatening. Similarly, the woman for whom 'rationality' was so important may not stop enjoying chess or problem-solving, but she may no longer feel that its inevitable inverse is so very great a threat to her. One can see how massive a threat to the founding desire of the Subject is posed by analysis, and it is not surprising that it encounters resistance. Do we truly want to give up our desires? Do we know what will take their place? Lacan was very far from sure about this: recognising desires was one thing, giving them up another. At the end, our greatest fear is probably that our desire will be replaced with the bland nothingness of nirvana; and yet, nirvana is exactly what is craved by those for whom the tension between desire and anxiety has become all too much; perhaps the only real solution is to recognise one's desire so as not to be enslaved by it.

Most analysis anyway stops at the point at which enough has been revealed for this tension to be reduced; there are many points at which an analysis can be ended, but the usual one is when the desire for emotional pain relief is too weak to keep the patient coming, when 'the analyst sees his own power decline, having been rendered useless by the demise of the symptoms and the completion of the personality'.[17]

Interpretation in Lacanian analysis

While the job of dialectisation and the construction of the signifying chain is the Subject's alone, and Lacanians tend to use interpretation far less than other analysts because of this, still the Lacanian analyst has also to interpret, if she/he is to fulfil his/her role as the Other.

If we remember that the symptom is classically seen to have meaning for the Subject, and bear in mind that interpretation is aimed at drawing out this meaning, what Lacan feared was that many classical psychoanalysts use interpretation as a kind of argument with which to persuade the patient to accept the meaning that the analyst has put upon it – a meaning built upon the analyst's theoretical constructs. '*You are being hostile towards me because you see me as the castrating father, who you were obliged to defend yourself against*', etc. If these interpretations encounter 'resistance', the analyst may employ more and more arguments out of his/her theoretical bible, to 'show' the patient how and why the interpretation works.

For Lacan, symptoms anyway have no 'real world' meaning that derives from a connection between a signifier and its signified, but come into being only from the effect of a signifier chain very particular and home-grown to the Subject (in fact, the *sinthome*), in which meaning comes from the Subject's own association of signifiers. Interpretations should therefore avoid introducing meaning determined by the analyst but aim at exposing the signifiers involved in the inscription of the *sinthome*, which is the structural basis for the symptom.

Lacan opposed the practice of telling your patient how their present emotions or actions fit into this or that theoretical construct, partly because such a practice suggests a lack of recognition on the part of the analyst that a construct is only that – a fiction of the analyst's imagination. Like all fictions, it can 'ring true' and be useful in allowing the patient to understand something, but equally, it may not, and may simply *be* untrue. But anyway, it is still an imaginary construct, and to respond to a patient's imaginary constructs (their fantasies) with one of your own is to play a game entirely within the Imaginary realm. Unless the analysand wants to become an analyst him/herself, or is of the kind of personality and intellect to which Lacanian theory will be interesting, he saw no direct treatment benefit in lecturing them about the Phallus, or the Thing, or the irruption of the Real. As for making interpretations in the way of the British, American, or Vienna Schools, Lacan had this to say: 'I will confine myself to remarking that, in reading the classical commentaries on interpretation, I always regret how little is made of the very facts people supply.'[18] In other words, if analysts weren't so busy trying to find in the patient's speech some basis for their theoretical constructs, and took greater literal account of what the Subject is saying, they might find the answers right there.

The worst effects of making interpretations by citing some piece of theory is that the patient might, especially if there is strong transference and a hysterical personality in question, begin to respond with fantasies constructed to fit that theoretical bases; the relationship between analyst and patient then becomes something of a *folie à deux*, which feeds off the Imaginary realms of both parties. And worst of all, in the case of hysterical patients, this game plays directly into the structure of the neurosis, which is that of wanting to fill one's inner emptiness with the desire of the Other. That this is so seems to be born out by the observation made in the 1950s of some analysts within the British school that the termination of an analysis was the point at which the patient comes to identify with the analyst. For Lacan, this seemed highly unsatisfactory: 'at best, the contemporary analyst leaves his patient at the point of purely imaginary identification – of which the hysteric remains captive, because her fantasy implies ensnarement in it'.[19]

In Lacanian analysis, interpretation is used sparingly, and not in reference to the analyst's theoretical constructs, except in particular circumstances, for instance, if the analysand has a good personal knowledge of Lacanian theory and is a trainee. More commonly, theory is, like counter-transference, the dummy in the game of bridge: one plays according to it but not with it. In other words, theory is there to help the analyst understand the patient and him/herself: it provides him/her with a model, a kind of code for use in decryption, but it is only a guidebook to the analyst's actions, and otherwise irrelevant to the process of analysis.

What was important for Lacan was that when an individual comes into analysis, it is in order to find the answers to certain questions posed by the circumstances of his/her life – answers that she/he already unconsciously knows, but to which his/her ego is oblivious. Lacan took the position that this was the only knowledge that really mattered; hence, his use of interpretation (or silence) was designed to help the Subject recognise the repressed knowledge *in their own way* and in the logic of their circumstances, and not according to a theoretical construct. 'If we conduct the Subject anywhere, it is to a deciphering which assumes that a sort of logic is already operative in the unconscious, a logic in which for example an interrogative voice or even the development of an argument can be recognised.'[20]

For Lacan, the only thing that determines whether an interpretation is correct or not is whether it is effective in the treatment. Obviously, a wrong interpretation will not work, but nor will a correct one if it is not couched in the right signifiers and delivered at precisely the right moment. An analyst may see some truth about the patient according to his/her theoretical system, but until the patient can see the same truth couched in the terms of his/her own reality, it is useless; after all, meaning can only be realised in the Subject's own construction of the signifier chain. It may be more useful to ask: when does one know that an interpretation has done the trick?

For Lacan, an interpretation is effective only if it works a transmutation in the patient – a transmutation that is visible *not* in the patient's immediate acceptance or rejection of the interpretation, but in an observable change manifested in the patient's future speech and actions. Lacan was not at all troubled by the patient's denying the accuracy of an interpretation – it would work its magic anyway if it was correct; nor was he pleased by the patient's agreeing with an interpretation, if nothing changed in his/her functioning afterwards. This is why he scoffed at the preoccupation of some analysts with 'negative transference', the drawer in which they put the patient's resistance to their interpretations: 'the subject's resistance, when it opposes suggestion, is but a desire to maintain desire. As such his resistance should be considered positive transference, since it is desire that maintains the direction of the analysis.'[21]

This is where, perhaps, a word could be said about the role of the analyst, and whether she/he allows his/her ego into play in the session. To Lacan, it was obvious that the answer was yes, but to many people this seemed to contradict, firstly, his assertion that the analyst must be 'pure mirror' and secondly, his recommendation that the analyst respond to the demands of the patient 'only from his position in the transference'. By the latter statement, he meant that interpretations should not involve arcane theories, but fit into the logic of the Subject's own discourse. By the former – well, the silence of the 'pure mirror' is necessary in order to allow the patient to associate freely and to start to form his/her signifier chain, but when it comes to interpretations, it was obvious (at least to Lacan) that it had to be the analyst's ego that spoke – what else could it be? Lacan pointed out that if the patient only received the analyst's speech as that of his/her imaginary interlocutor in the transference, then the patient would remain indefinitely within the same position and the analysis would remain frozen in time. Furthermore, in making the interpretation, the analyst had to re-assume his/her ego in order to fulfil his/her other role – that of the Subject-supposed-to-know, which is also the Other.

As an aside, Lacan seemed rather irritated at the fussing over what the analyst was supposed to be when making an interpretation: 'Who will say what the analyst is there, and what remains of him when he is up against the wall of the task of interpreting?' To avoid the bland answer that he (the analyst) is a man, and an animal of our species, he recasts the question more directly a few paragraphs later: '*Who is speaking?*' – for which the answer has to be '*Me*' (with all the double meaning of the French '*moi*' as 'ego').[22]

Lacan was also rare in that he made a real effort to understand *how* interpretation works. Most others are content merely to note its efficacy, or lack thereof (and in the latter case to attribute its failure to 'resistance' on the part of the patient), but this is like believing in magic: it works, but we don't know how. Few analysts have made hypotheses about *how* interpretation works, and Lacan is rather damning of the efforts of Edward Glover in this direction, who 'finds interpretation everywhere, even in the banality of a medical prescription, being unable to set any limits to it … Conceived of in this way, interpretation becomes a sort of phlogiston; it is manifest in everything that is understood rightly or wrongly, as long as it feeds the flame of the imaginary.'[23]

The effects of a well-done interpretation are observable in the patient, but this gives rise to many other questions, the first being what exactly has changed and how? Lacan chose to work from the second question, the 'how', and felt that the answer lay in the nature of the material being worked, which is speech. 'No index suffices to show where interpretation operates, unless one accepts in all its radical implications a concept of the function of the signifier, which grasps where it is that the subject subordinates himself to the signifer to so great an extent that he is suborned [taken control of] by it.'[24]

Lacan postulated that the analyst, having been attributed the role of the Other, who is the keeper of the treasury of signifiers and knowledge, is designated the role of supplying the missing links in the signifier chain that the Subject is forming.

> In order to decipher the diachrony of unconscious repetitions, interpretation must introduce into the synchrony of signifiers that come together there something that suddenly makes translation possible – this is precisely what is allowed by the function of the Other in the possession of the code, it being in relation to that Other that the missing element appears.[25]

It is not the patient's belief in the analyst that makes the analyst able to supply the right link, but it is certainly this belief that allows the analysand to hear and recognise it, should the analyst be good enough to produce it.

'Making an interpretation' is a highly delicate manoeuvre which needs precision timing and the use of exactly the right words. For example, in the search for the signifying chain of the Subject's truth, the analyst may have been aware for some time of the Subject's master signifiers, having heard them often or deduced them from what she/he has heard; however, there is another step to be made towards finding their repressed counterparts, and if and when the analyst has an idea what these are, it is best to gently push the analysand towards enunciating them him/herself, perhaps with a well-timed question, or just a single word when the analysand is groping for it, and very nearly has it. To mention it too soon would lead to instant dismissal and denegation, and not to seize upon it at the right moment would also allow it to be re-interred in a welter of covering signifiers.

As Lacan pointed out, the analytical transference not only allows for the opening up of the shutters behind which the truth is hidden, but it also allows them to be slammed tight, by exactly the same process of discourse. This is why he warns against analysing and explaining transference as a means of interpretation – it calls into play too much of the patient's ego:

> To appeal to some healthy part of the Subject thought to be there ... capable of judging with the analyst what is happening in the transference, is to misunderstand that it is precisely this part ... that closes the door, or the window, or the shutters or whatever – and that the beauty with whom one wishes to speak is there, behind, only too willing to open the shutters again. This is why it is at this moment that interpretation becomes decisive, for it is to the beauty that one must speak ... the unconscious is the discourse of the Other. Now, the discourse of the Other that is to be realised, that of the unconscious, is not beyond the closure, it is outside. It is this discourse which, through the mouth of the analyst, calls for the reopening of the shutter.[26]

In conclusion

Lacan saw analysis as a perilous adventure best embarked upon out of a sense of desperation; any other reason for starting it is not as likely to achieve as good a result, unless one's desire was very strong indeed. For Lacan, the desire for truth and for knowledge was the ultimate desire, whose pursuit produced the ultimate enjoyment. Analysis should therefore not aim at any clumsy excision of the desire of the Subject, but rather its strengthening; it should not strengthen the ego, but weaken its fictions. For him, the desire of the Subject would and should always remain elusive, and the adventure would only get better as one approached it.

> The question of the realisation of desire is always formulated from the point of view of a Last Judgement. Try to imagine

what 'to have realised one's desire' might mean, if it is not to have it realised, so to speak, in the end. It's this trespassing of death upon life that gives its dynamism to any question that attempts to find a formulation for the Subject of the realisation of desire.[27]

13

After the flood
Lacan in the twenty-first century

Let us hope it will last!
(Maria-Letizia Ramolino, Napoleon's mother)

It is now more than a quarter of a century since the death of
Lacan; the generation of analysts who were themselves on his
couch or who attended his seminars is now the 'old guard'. For
some of them to have been able to move away from the position
of absolute respect for the master and to even disagree with some
of his ideas probably indicates some kind of resolution of their
transference. The next generation will not have experienced the
same transference (although some transference can and will exist
even with a dead Subject, still writ large in his discourse) and are
better able to take an objective view of his work and perhaps
build upon it. However, there will always be those even in the
new generation who are searching for an absolute master, or
who want to become an absolute master and see in Lacan's
complex writings a powerful tool to impress and control the
non- or less initiated.

The death of Jacques Lacan left his followers in an institutional and a theoretical crisis that led to the fracturing of the
group. Beyond the political and personal aspects of these
conflicts, there were theoretical differences that divided Lacan's
followers into two broad camps (a third, which had splintered
from the main group before his death, could be said to exist in
the form of the Organisation Psychanalytique de Langue
Française (OPLF)).

The first comprises those analysts who tend to see Lacan's theory as a finished body of work, which needs only to be commented upon, explained to newcomers, and taught to pupils. These followers tend to believe that there is a unifying theory in Lacan's work that close study will reveal. The other group takes the view that just as Lacan's theories built upon Freud, his own followers and subsequent generations should continue to build upon his works, even if in doing so they may move away from some of his formulations. This anti-doctrinaire group is somewhat closer to the spirit of Jacques Lacan, who never claimed to have a unifying theory, and believed that the theory of psychoanalysis was a work in progress. Some of these analysts could be named 'Modern Lacanians', in parallel to what has happened in the Freudian sphere. These differences apply to individual analysts rather than schools or institutions, and there are people of both types in the various Lacanian organisations.

In France, Charles Melman and Jean Bergès are probably the most interesting representatives of this second group; what is interesting about them on the world stage is that both of them, like Lacan, are psychiatrists. Outside of France, psychiatry has become very alienated from psychoanalysis, to the impoverishment of both disciplines. It should be remembered that both Freud and Lacan were doctors, and that many of the major psychoanalytical insights of the pioneers of the science were the result of clinical observation in hospitals. The fact that psychiatry deals with extreme cases, as well as psychiatric manifestations with a bodily cause, allows its practitioners a breadth and depth of view not available to analysts who deal principally with a self-selected and voluntary group of analysands. The small group of Lacanian *psychiatrists* that remains in France is in the privileged position of the founders of their science and their contributions should not be neglected.

Charles Melman has built upon Lacan's work, treating it as part of the canon of psychoanalytic theory, which is the greater work in progress. Having devoted a lot of his work to the theory of psychosis and obsessional neurosis, he also used psychoanalytical concepts to understand changes in society, as Freud did in *Civilisation and Its Discontents*.[1] Another major author within the group of modern Lacanians is Jean Bergès. As a Child and Adolescent Psychiatrist with a solid experience of Neurology and Paediatrics, he was also one of very few psychoanalysts interested in the body, and who practised relaxation therapy. His awareness of the physical-psychological interconnections gave him a very particular kind of insight into human development. During his seminars at St. Anne Hospital he introduced several new concepts, and developed new ways of understanding old ones. One of these new concepts is of the operation of bodily functions as the blueprint for the thinking process. Another of Bergès' advances is the use he made of Transitivism, a very old psychiatric concept denoting the process whereby someone imagines another person to be experiencing the same thing that she/he is experiencing. Bergès, after Wallon and Lacan, saw the process of Transitivism at the heart of the interactions that lead to the kindling of thinking in children. Transitivism is the mechanism that helps the mother make hypotheses about the baby. The game of hypothesis between the mother and the baby is the beginning of 'social interaction' and allows the child to access the Symbolic register. He also offered a new meta-psychological approach to what the English-speaking world tends to call the autistic spectrum.[2]

Will Lacan's legacy last? Two points have to be examined separately: the future of the Lacanian model within psychoanalysis and the future of psychoanalysis within the broader spectrum of 'psychological therapies'.

In the context of the first point, Lacanian psychoanalysis has grown rather like yeast in a warm room. The first Lacanian school was created in the early 1960s, and subsequently split and split again, with each schism resulting in the birth of a new school with its own energy and vigour, so that at the beginning of the twenty-first century, there are probably at least as many if not more Lacanian analysts than those of any other theoretical orientation. The IPA does not recognise the schools from which these analysts have emerged, but this has not stopped them functioning. However, this lack of a single regulatory body has made it difficult to put hard figures to the numbers of Lacanian analysts practising today. In 1992, the Association Mondiale de Psychanalyse was created to regroup some of the Lacanian schools; the fact of its necessity could be seen a sign of the health of these groups while at the same time perpetuating a position of competition with the IPA.

However, the strength of Lacan's work lies not with political power: Lacanian analysts are typically uninterested in seizing this, or even in questions of what is 'mainstream', 'popular', or otherwise. Anti-institutionalism is an inherent part of Lacan's legacy, and he cast this as one of the founding tenets of his theory, in his Four Discourses. The enduring success of Lacan is in the usefulness of his theory itself. Through his clever intuitions, careful observations, and borrowings from other sciences, Lacan created an edifice of great explanatory potential that analysts have found effective in understanding complex issues. Gender issues, transference, trauma, the role of fathers, and psychosis are among the many topics that can be re-examined through his theoretical construct.

Lacan's legacy

Lacan's work is like Freud's, a work in progress: he went as far as he could during his lifetime and many issues he raised can and should be developed further. This allows a vast scope of work for generations of analysts, who could and should emulate Lacan in using advances made in other fields such as linguistics and philosophy to re-examine Lacanian concepts, in the same way that Lacan reworked Freudian ones. Lacan's ideas on the practice of analysis are also of great relevance, as they arose from genuine issues encountered by practitioners that were not properly discussed in the analytical institutions, and which have remained unaddressed to this day. For example, there has never been a theoretical debate about the duration of the analytical session – and now there is more than a quarter of a century's worth of experience of the use of variable duration sessions to add to the discussion. Likewise, the question of the training and accreditation of an analyst has never been debated in depth, perhaps for historical and political reasons; but the debate initiated in the second part of the twentieth century should at some stage take place in the twenty-first.

One factor in Lacan's longevity is the fact that because of his 'borrowings' from linguistics, philosophy, and anthropology, his work can be and is used by academics in non-clinical fields. Literature, sociology, politics, gender studies, and other fields involving critical thinking (e.g. film or theatre studies) all make use of Lacanian theory. Lacan's work is studied by philosophers, and his complex views still fuel many debates among scholars. The amount of this non-clinical interest in Lacan is vast and a simple internet search on Lacan's key concepts reveals a world of scholarly work. The wide-ranging nature of Lacan's popularity is in some way a guarantee of the survival of his work, as it places it beyond the vagaries of psychoanalytical and psychological fashion as dictated by an establishment which has from the outset been prone to political wranglings, and to the sudden embracing or rejecting of particular theories. The applicability of Lacan in far more than psychoanalysis should ensure that the future of his work remains firmly linked to its intellectual merit.

Having said this, it remains sad that Lacan, the psychiatrist, is rarely read by psychiatrists. This is probably in part the result of the move towards a very biological model of psychiatry that began with the development of the first generation of psychotropic drugs in the 1960s, and which was granted 'official' status with the publication of the *Diagnostic Statistical Manual* (*DSM III*) classification in 1980. This is the psychiatric classification system of the American Psychiatric Association and has become the dominant model worldwide. It involved a paradigm shift which left very little place for psychological models in the understanding of mental disorders, and even less for the most complicated elements of this understanding – psychoanalysis. Within psychoanalysis, the difficulty of Lacanian texts and the problems of translation have led to his being simply left out of any standard teaching.

The future of psychoanalysis

It is an unfortunate but incontrovertible truth that the standing of any therapeutic system in society is based largely on economics. At the beginning of the twenty-first century, the United Kingdom (along with many other countries with publicly funded health services) is preoccupied with 'evidence-based' practices, which are thought to guarantee value for money; and the scientifically demonstrated efficacy of cognitive-behavioural therapies (CBT) has brought about a revival of interest in psychological therapies. The psychoanalytical establishment has not yet attempted to justify its existence by means of statistics to show efficacy, and is hampered in this by theoretical difficulties in defining what is a good 'result'. But it may not be long before it does take on the challenge, and then one of the issues that will arise is that of what happens to a patient in the long term. Arguments are bound to rage over whether the disappearance of a symptom for a six-month period is a real 'result', and whether the resurgence of different symptoms later on disproves it. However, what is interesting for psychoanalysts in the proof of efficacy that CBT has undertaken to provide is that CBT is, at least, a *psychological* therapy and does not fit the neurological/ genetic models of mental disorder used by a large number of psychiatrists these days; the success of CBT may push the latter group to rethink the assumptions that underlie the *DSM*.

CBT originated in the United States as a radically different therapy from psychoanalysis and in opposition to it, but the two disciplines are curiously similar in many fundamental ways. Firstly, like psychoanalysis, CBT depends upon a belief that psychological suffering and dysfunctionality can be alleviated by a purely psychological intervention. Secondly, the medium used to understand and address the suffering is language. Thirdly, the treatment mechanism takes the form of sessions during which two individuals in asymmetrical positions interact – the therapist, because of his/her knowledge, directs the treatment and decides when it ends. The practitioner must be aware of and take into account the patient's attitude towards the treatment and also towards him/herself, and must pay similar attention to his/her own attitude towards the patient, as this could interfere negatively with the success of the treatment. With very minor rephrasing, all of this looks very similar to some of the tenets of psychoanalysis. It is therefore possible that far from being undermined by the rise of CBT, psychoanalysis will in the long term benefit from it.

Similarly, it may be precisely the differences between CBT and psychoanalysis that ensure the lasting success of the latter model. The two approaches differ strongly on several points, the first of which is the attitude towards symptoms, and the second, the question of the unconscious. CBT puts the reduction of symptoms as its main aim, while psychoanalysis tends to focus on understanding the cause of the symptom. Without going into the merits of either position, it is likely that both approaches will suit different people in different types of difficulty. A person who wants only to quickly reduce their fear of public spaces would probably seek help from a CBT practitioner, while someone who wants to understand the root causes of their miserable love-life may seek help from a psychoanalyst.

CBT is based on a theory that it is not events in themselves that upset us, but the meanings we give them. However, CBT believes that this meaning is conscious, can be accessed, and is not ambiguous. If someone says that they feel sorry for a person, they do feel sorry and it is possible that their problem is that they should not; the therapist then tries to help the patient to see that they are thinking about something in the 'wrong way'. The concept of the unconscious, a central Freudian discovery, renders the picture instantly more complex: if you say you are sorry for someone it *might* indeed mean that you are sorry, but could also mean that you can't face your own aggressiveness and the fact that you are delighted at what happened to the other. The question of the existence of the unconscious is crucial, because if CBT starts to take into account the possibility of unconscious meanings and logic, then it would become another branch of psychoanalysis.

Perhaps the greater threat to psychoanalysis is the rise of various forms of 'counselling'. This is a career that has emerged from diverse roots and in which there is at present no legal minimum qualification necessary for practising. Training is very varied, with some courses providing quite in-depth and valuable education, but others rather sketchy programmes. There has been a strong self-help, 'mutual support', and 'client-based' element in the evolution of the field, which means that from the very outset, the individual in counselling can expect a 'sympathetic' approach; she/he is presumed to be an 'offended party', a 'victim', and 'sinned against' rather than directly responsible for his/her problem. It would be wrong to tar all counsellors with the same brush, as it is a field encompassing extremely varied theoretical bases and practices, and as there are some very good and talented counsellors around; but the semi-professional nature of the field allows it also to hide a multitude of sins. In its least desirable form, counselling tends to strengthen the individual's neurotic defences, trying for example to increase 'assertiveness' and 'self-esteem', and to support what Lacan would say was the 'fiction of the ego'. Counselling has become popular in the United Kingdom, where it is available on the public purse because it is relatively inexpensive, and it is better that individuals in need of support get some rather than none at all; after all, the very fact of being listened to by an uninvolved party has a therapeutic function. However, there is a danger of counselling being used in place of more formalised and rigorous therapies where the latter is necessary, and with budgetary concerns outstripping human ones, this is unfortunately increasingly the case.

However, differences in opinion between psychoanalysts, cognitive-behavioural therapists, and counsellors are ultimately less important than those between all these people and those who do not believe in any psychological therapies at all. And because there is a radical opposition between those who see mental and even emotional problems as just the result of biological factors (genetics, invisible lesions in the brain, etc.) and therefore treatable by chemical and physical means, and those who see them as resulting from psychological factors, the future of Lacanian theory will always be linked with that of other schools of psychoanalysis and also of all psychological therapies. In a fiercely competitive therapeutic market-place, it may seem very optimistic (or perhaps even insane) to predict a bright future for a therapy characterised by its refusal to justify itself as a 'quick fix', its doubts as to whether 'curing' is actually a desirable goal, and which does not even guarantee sessions of a set duration. Lacanian analysis is like the bumblebee, which should not fly and yet does. It attracts more and more psychoanalysts, and these analysts, more and more patients, perhaps because these individuals have experienced for themselves that it works, or because what they have heard of it has the ring of truth for them. Also, clinicians may be attracted to it because it is a work in progress, which leaves them the possibility of developing the theory further. As suggested in chapter 12, Lacanian patients are a self-selecting group: they are not people who want a quick cure for a specific symptom but those in search of deep truths and insights. However, it must also be said that this does not preclude Lacanian practice from being useful to all manner of patients, from the most extreme clinical cases of psychosis to the mildest neurotics. Whether practitioners who have to deal with such patients in their daily work (e.g. psychiatrists) will become more interested in Lacanian ideas will depend upon the dissemination of the ideas through publications and academic institutions. At present, it is only in France that Lacan has a place in psychiatry and clinical psychology, probably because, until recently, his work was not translated into the current *lingua franca* (English); this is a first hurdle that is being gradually overcome. The second is the difficulty of explaining his theory, but as with the first point, recent years have seen the publication of more and more books that seek to do this, of which this is one. These efforts at explanation, the success of Lacanian analysis in practice, and the theoretical work of the Modern Lacanians, should together ensure that the work of this abstruse, infuriating, brilliant, and honest thinker continues to bear fruit for all time.

Notes

Introduction

1. Jacques Lacan 1966. *Ecrits*. Paris, Editions du Seuil. Bruce Fink's English translation is also referred to: 2006, in collaboration with Héloïse Fink and Russell Grigg. New York, Norton. Notes indicate whether quotations are my own translation of the French text, or Fink's version.

Chapter 1

1. 'The Mirror Stage', 1936. Published as 'La Stade du miroir comme formateur de la fonction du Je, telle quelle nous est révélé dans l'experience psychanalytique', in *Ecrits* (French version).

Chapter 2

1. 'The Mirror Stage', *Ecrits*, own translation.
2. '*Identification* contrasts with *imitation* not simply as the *global assimilation* of a structure, but as the *virtual assimilation of development* implied by that structure in a still undifferentiated state' ('Beyond the Reality Principle', *Ecrits*, trans. Bruce Fink). In other words, imitating someone is merely copying how they are at the present moment, while identification is an assimilation of their personality structure so that you develop as they would, and will in future react according to the same underlying structure to situations the object of identification may never have encountered, in a way that she/he might.
3. 'The Mirror Stage', *Ecrits*, trans. Bruce Fink.
4. 'The Mirror Stage', *Ecrits*, own translation.
5. 'The Mirror Stage', *Ecrits*, trans. Bruce Fink.
6. Joël Dor 1985. *Introduction à la lecture de Lacan*. Paris, Denoël.

Chapter 3

1. *Seminar XI, The Four Fundamental Concepts of Psychoanalysis*, trans. Alan Sheridan 2004 (1977). New York, Karnac. Originally published as *Les Quatre Concepts fondamentaux de la psychanalyse, Le séminaire, Livre XI*, 1972. Paris, Seuil.
2. Susanne K. Langer 1951 (1942). 'The Logic of Signs and Symbols', in *Philosophy in a New Key: A Study in the Symbolism of Reason, Rite and Art*. Cambridge, MA, Harvard University Press.
3. Roman Jakobson 1956. 'Two Aspects of Language and Two Types of Aphasic Disturbances', in *Fundamentals of Language*, R. Jakobson and M. Halle (eds). The Hague, Mouton.

Chapter 4

1. 'The Direction of the Treatment and the Principles of its Power', *Ecrits*, trans. Bruce Fink.

Chapter 5

1. The quote is from Lacan's *Seminar V: Les formations de l'inconscient, 1957–58*; Seuil 1998; own translation.
2. Ibid.
3. Dor 1985.
4. The type of depression defined by René Spitz in 1945 in his study of hospitalised children which arises from the removal of the child's main source of support, now called an attachment object.

Chapter 6

1. Roland Chemama 1995. *Dictionnaire de la psychanalyse*. Paris, Larousse.
2. Seminar on 'The Purloined Letter', *Ecrits*, own translation.
3. Own translation of *Le Moi dans la théorie de Freud et dans la technique de la psychanalyse, Le séminaire, Livre II*, 1978 (1954). Paris, Seuil.
4. Chemama 1995.

5. 'Reponse au commentaire de Jean Hyppolite sur la "Verneinung" de Freud', *Ecrits*, own translation.
6. *Seminar II*, own translation.
7. 'The Function and Field of Speech in Psychoanalysis', *Ecrits*, own translation.
8. Bruce Fink 1995. *The Lacanian Subject: Between Language and Jouissance*. Princeton, NJ, Princeton University Press.
9. Seminar on 'The Purloined Letter', *Ecrits*, own translation.
10. Chemama 1995.
11. *Seminar VII, The Ethics of Psychoanalysis*, trans. Dennis Porter 1992. London, Routledge.
12. *Les Formations de l'inconscient, Le séminaire, Livre V*, 1998. Paris, Seuil, own translation.
13. *Seminar XI*, trans. Alan Sheridan.

Chapter 7

1. 'The Direction of the Treatment and the Principle of its Power', *Ecrits*, trans. Bruce Fink.
2. Ibid.
3. 'La Subversion du sujet et la dialectique du désir', *Ecrits*, own translation.
4. 'La Signification du Phallus', *Ecrits*, own translation.
5. *Seminar XI*, trans. Alan Sheridan.
6. Sigmund Freud 1975 (first English translation 1922). *Beyond the Pleasure Principle*. London, Norton.
7. *Seminar XI*, trans. Alan Sheridan.
8. *Seminar XVII*, own translation of *Envers de la Psychanalyse, Le séminaire, Livre 17*, 1991. Paris, Seuil.
9. *Seminar XI*, trans. Alan Sheridan.
10. 'The Direction of the Treatment and the Principles of its Power', *Ecrits*, trans. Bruce Fink.
11. 'The Subversion of the Subject and the Dialectic of Desire', *Ecrits*, trans. Bruce Fink.
12. 'La Subversion du sujet et la dialectique du désir', *Ecrits*, own translation.

13. Ibid.
14. 'The Direction of the Treatment and the Principles of its Power', *Ecrits*, trans. Bruce Fink.

Chapter 8

1. *Seminar VI, Desire and its Interpretation*, 1959, own translation of *Le Désir et son interpretation, Le séminaire, Livre 6*. Association Lacanienne Internationale, documents hors commerce a l'usage des members (not for sale documents, for members' use only).

2. Plato's *Symposium*, trans. Benjamin Jowett. An unabridged revision by Albert A. Anderson is available: 2003. Millis, MA, Agora Publications.

3. 'The Subversion of the Subject and the Dialectic of Desire', *Ecrits*, trans. Bruce Fink.

4. What I have chosen to call 'lack-cause-of-anxiety' Lacan calls the *manque a être* or 'lack-in-being'; I have avoided this term because to readers unused to Lacan's mode of expression, it comes across as unnecessarily mystical (in fact it derives from philosophical theories about Being and Meaning). A 'lack that causes anxiety' is at least clear, and stands in matching contrast to the 'object cause of desire'.

5. Jean-Pierre Cléro 2006, p. 144. *Y a-t-il une philosophie de Lacan?* Paris, Ellipses.

6. Freud postulated two 'principles' between which there exists a tension in the human psyche: the pleasure principle, which governs various childish activities, and the reality principle, which intervenes to direct activities towards a satisfactory 'real-world' goal. He maintained that the pleasure principle came first, and as the child comes to understand the demands and laws of the real world, its psychological well-being depends upon treading a course between the two principles.

7. *Seminar VII*, trans. Dennis Porter, p.65.

8. Ibid.

9. Ibid.

Chapter 9

1. *Seminar XVIII*, own translation of *D'un Discours qui ne serait pas du semblant, Le séminaire, Livre XVIII'*. Association Lacanienne Internationale, documents a l'usage des members (not for sale documents, for members' use only).

Chapter 11

1. 'Lacan 1969. Jacques Proposition du 9 Octobre 1967 Sur le Psychanalyste de l'Ecole', *Scilicet* No. 1. Paris, Seuil.
2. L'Orientation Lacanienne, 'la Formation'. From the Ecole de la Cause Freudienne website, www.causefreudienne.org.

Chapter 12

1. Alain Didier-Weill 2001. *Quarier Lacan*. Flammarion, Paris.
2. Gérard Hadad 2002. *Le Jour où Lacan m'a adopté*. Grasset, Paris.
3. 'Fonction et champ de la parole et du langage', *Ecrits*, own translation.
4. Melanie Klein 1952. 'The Origins of Transference'. *International Journal of Psychoanalysis*, 33: 433–8.
5. 'The Direction of the Treatment and the Principle of its Power', *Ecrits*, trans. Bruce Fink.
6. Dor 1985.
7. 'The Direction of the Treatment and the Principles of its Power', *Ecrits*, own translation.
8. *Seminar XI*, own translation.
9. 'The Direction of the Treatment and the Principle of its Power', *Ecrits*, trans. Bruce Fink.
10. 'Intervention sur le transfert', *Ecrits*, own translation.
11. *Seminar I, Freud's Papers on Technique, 1953–4*, own translation of Lacan, *Ecrits Techniques, Le séminaire, Livre 1*. Association Lacanienne Internationale, documents hors commerce a l'usage des members (not for sale documents, for members' use only).

12. 'The Direction of the Treatment and the Principle of its Power', *Ecrits*, trans. Bruce Fink.
13. *Seminar XI*, own translation.
14. 'Variations on the Standard Treatment', *Ecrits*, own translation.
15. Ibid.
16. Ibid.
17. 'Beyond the Reality Principle', *Ecrits*, trans. Bruce Fink.
18. 'The Direction of the Treatment and the Principle of its Power', *Ecrits*, trans. Bruce Fink.
19. Ibid.
20. 'The Subversion of the Subject and the Dialectic of Desire', *Ecrits*, trans. Bruce Fink.
21. 'The Direction of the Treatment and the Principle of its Power', *Ecrits*, trans. Bruce Fink.
22. Ibid.
23. Ibid. Phlogiston was thought to be a fundamental substance – an element – that was released in combustion; oddly, this erroneous idea continued very late in the history of science, and was used to explain away the inexplicable up until the late eighteenth century.
24. 'The Direction of the Treatment and the Principles of its Power', *Ecrits*, trans. Bruce Fink.
25. Ibid.
26. *Seminar XI*, trans. Alan Sheridan.
27. *Seminar VII*, trans. Dennis Porter.

Chapter 13

1. Charles Melman 2002. *L'Homme sans gravité – La Jouissance à tout prix*. Paris, Denoël.
2. Jean Bergès and Gabriel Balbo 2001. *Psychose, autisme et disharmonie cognitive*. Paris, Eres.

Glossary

1. *Seminar VII*, trans. Dennis Porter.

Glossary

agalma   a Greek ornamental offering to the gods, which may be a sign of power and object for transmission or exchange. In Plato's *Symposium*, the *agalma* is contained within the person of Socrates, who is portrayed as ugly and of no physical value. Lacan uses the *agalma*, which is the precious property contained within something whose only value derives from being its container, as a metaphor for the ***objet petit a*** – the object cause of desire – which is the quality of desirability to be found in otherwise valueless objects.

anaclytic   the property of *leaning on* something. Anaclytic depression is the type defined by René Spitz in 1945 in his study of hospitalised children, which arises from the removal of the child's main source of support, now called an attachment object.

l'autre (**the other**)   what the child at the Mirror Stage first identifies as itself in the mirror. This is often referred to as 'the small other' in English and '*le petit autre*' in French to emphasise the fact that it is written with a lower-case 'o' or 'a', which distinguishes it from ***l'Autre*** or **the Other**. The importance of the concept of the small other is that the child's identification with it forms a template for its relations with other people, now that it has 'recognised' itself as one among them.

l'Autre (**the Other**)   the set of rules and hypotheses into which the Subject is born. Manifestations of the Other are language and all other symbolic constructs.

castration   the symbolic loss of an imaginary object, the **Phallus**. Castration is the acceptance that one is less than perfect, limited, not all-powerful and able to control or satisfy the world. Castration is therefore a symbolic process which allows the child to situate itself within the Law, and to accept that its own desires are not paramount. Castration is the central source of neurotic anxiety.

desire   the result of the failure of speech to express what the Subject lacks.

desire (of the analyst)   what the analyst expects the analysand to achieve, and which supports the analytical process.

discourse   what is said by someone, which is determined by the particularities of the Subject in its relationship with **signifiers** and objects.

foreclosure   to foreclose is to close beforehand – to bar access absolutely. When applied to the paternal metaphor, foreclosure is the failure of the Subject to 'cross the bar of metaphor' and thereby to access the realm of the **Symbolic**. For Lacan, foreclosure formed the basis of psychosis.

Imaginary   one of Lacan's three 'realms' or orders of the psyche; in this text, capitalised to distinguish it from the commonplace use of 'imaginary'. The Imaginary is named for the mental processes that issue from the encounter between the infant and its image in the mirror; it is the realm of the senses in that it houses the conceptions that issue directly from sensorial perception. Because of the **Mirror Stage**, it is also the order of conceptualisations and functioning that proceeds *from the body's image*.

jouissance   usually translated as 'enjoyment' or 'usage' in English. In Lacanian thought, *jouissance* has the advantage of denoting *not* the satisfaction that arises from the attainment of a goal, but a form of enjoyment derived from the usage of something in its legitimate (intended) way – the pleasure that comes with the functioning of the physical or psychological apparatus associated with a drive. This distinguishes this type of enjoyment from the pleasure obtained from the satisfaction of a need, which, unlike *jouissance*, reduces tension.

matheme a formula for expressing a psychoanalytical concept in pseudo-mathematical form. A matheme should hold true for all variables within it.

méconnaissance this has in other works been translated as 'misrecognition', but this term implies that something has been wrongly recognised. I believe that what Lacan meant by it was 'obliviousness', as in having a 'blind spot' with regard to something. Hence, the Subject may be oblivious to its own intentions or meanings.

Mirror Stage the point in the child's development at which it recognises its own image in the mirror, which marks an importance step in the formation of the Subject. At this point, the infant moves from perceiving itself in a fragmented way to having a unified image of itself as an entity.

Name-of-the-Father the **signifier** that comes to stand for the **Phallus** in the paternal metaphor.

l'objet petit a the object cause of desire.

la passe a process by which Lacanian analysts were judged for accreditation. Lacan invented this process to try to overcome some of the weaknesses in the accreditation process of other schools of psychoanalysis. In *la passe*, the candidate has to give an account of his/her analysis and what she/he has understood to two other people, who then 'report' to a jury, describing what they have heard.

Phallus signifier associated with the idea of the object of the mother's desire and therefore a supposed 'perfect object', which becomes the object of primary repression, and which is a precursor of the *objet petit a*.

Real   one of the 'realms' or 'orders' of the psyche. The Real is what is expelled when a **signifier** becomes attached to some morsel of reality; it is the bit that the signifier fails to capture. For everything that comes into our field of recognition by means of a signifier, something of it must remain imperceptible, unsymbolised. This is the Real.

sexuation   the way in which men and women relate to their own gender and to questions of castration and gender difference.

signified   the idea that is represented by a word – half of the Saussurian linguistic sign.

signifier   the signal that carries an idea to form a word; in linguistics, a sound-image – half of the Saussurian linguistic sign.

sinthome   an aspect of the Subject's structure, which produces symptoms through the action of the specific configuration of its signifier chain on the Real. It is represented as a fourth circle on the Borromean knot, holding the **Imaginary** with the **Symbolic** and **Real**.

Symbolic   a 'realm' or 'order' of the psyche, which holds language, the Other – all the rules and hypotheses that organise human society and thought. The unconscious also belongs to the realm of the Symbolic, as it is constituted of repressed **signifiers**.

the Thing   a formulation of Freud's to describe what is 'characterised by the fact that it is impossible for us to imagine'; it is the object of loss, which attracts desire, although it is not itself the object of desire. For Lacan, the Thing exists outside of language and the **Symbolic** – it is 'the first thing that separated itself from everything the subject began to name and articulate';[1] he also equates it with the forbidden aspect of the mother.

topology   the branch of mathematics that studies the properties of a space that are preserved under continuous deformations. Because it involves finding properties that remain constant no matter how much the *appearance* of the space changes, it is an attractive model to a psychoanalyst looking for consistency of factors in the bewildering complexity of the human psyche and its interactions.

Index

Note: Page references in italics indicate diagrams; those in bold type indicate Glossary entries.